SACRIFICE

www.penguin.co.uk

Sacrifice

A Year in the Life of a Champion Jockey

OISIN MURPHY

bantam

TRANSWORLD PUBLISHERS

UK | USA | Canada | Ireland | Australia
India | New Zealand | South Africa

Transworld is part of the Penguin Random House group of companies
whose addresses can be found at global.penguinrandomhouse.com.

Penguin Random House UK, One Embassy Gardens,
8 Viaduct Gardens, London SW11 7BW

penguin.co.uk

Penguin
Random House
UK

First published in Great Britain in 2025 by Bantam
an imprint of Transworld Publishers

001

Typeset in 13/16pt Minion Pro by Six Red Marbles UK, Thetford, Norfolk
Printed and bound in Great Britain by Clays Ltd, Elcograf S.p.A.

The authorized representative in the EEA is Penguin Random House Ireland,
Morrison Chambers, 32 Nassau Street, Dublin D02 YH68.

A CIP catalogue record for this book is available from the British Library.

ISBN:
9780857507587

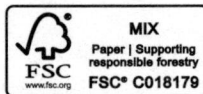

SACRIFICE

Contents

Beginnings

BECAUSE HORSE RACING IS A continuous and frag-
mented global sporting behemoth, deciding when to start
this book of mine, which I hope will offer you the reader an
interesting and entertaining insight into the day-to-day life
of a sometimes frighteningly obsessive professional jockey,
has caused me no end of worry. I'm not half as good at
making decisions as I am at fretting, and so consulting me on
what might be an appropriate point in time to kick off the
proceedings was an act that I only wish the publishers had
tried harder to resist. The end of the previous season? The
Breeders' Cup? Christmas? New Year's Day? The Lincoln
meeting at Doncaster?

'Let me get back to you,' I said to them eventually. 'I need
to have a think.'

Had this book simply been about my quest to become
champion jockey again, which I only decided to go for in
March, then the start of the Flat Jockeys Championship
would have been ideal. It isn't though. This book is an honest
account of how a deeply flawed young man from the small
town of Killarney in the south-west of Ireland, who it's fair

to say has led a fairly eventful life so far, copes with being a jockey and copes with being himself. And I'm not sure which is the most hazardous, to be honest. When we're not racing we're often starving ourselves as jockeys and when we are racing we're always being followed by an ambulance. Those two quite sobering facts speak volumes when it comes to demonstrating the precariousness of what we do for a living.

My own personal form of jeopardy comes in the shape of a self-destruct button. A self-destruct button that's omnipresent and varies in size depending on how things are going for me generally and how I'm feeling inside. I'm not sure which is worse. I'll tell you one thing though, both tend to keep me well and truly on my toes.

A fourteen-month ban and £31,000 fine that I received at the start of 2022 for breaching Covid travel protocols and for failing two breath tests is by far the most infamous result of me pressing my self-destruct button.

In terms of breaching Covid protocols, which accounted for the £31,000 fine and eleven of the fourteen months, it all began on 24 August 2020 when the stewards at Ayr found me guilty of careless riding and banned me for seven days. Initially I was going to appeal the decision but then decided to take a short holiday instead with my girlfriend to the Greek island of Mykonos.

A few days into the holiday the island was moved on to the global pandemic red list which meant that on my return I would have to self-isolate for 14 days, which I'm afraid I did not. I just kept on racing as normal. The lying started before that though. While in Mykonos I was committed to doing a vlog for Sporting Life and as it was pretty evident I wasn't in Lambourn I told them that I was at Lake Como, which at the time wasn't on the red list. I didn't think much of it. I was just getting myself out of a fix.

Over the next year or so, as suspicion grew about my true whereabouts during that week, I was given probably hundreds of opportunities to come clean. But the longer it went on, the harder it was to tell the truth. Lying to people became the norm and there were times when I almost believed what I was saying. What initially had been a stupid error of judgement that would no doubt have been dealt with swiftly by the BHA had turned into a monster. A monster that over time involved dozens of people and would end up almost destroying my reputation and career. It was and still is the biggest mistake of my life so far.

With regards to the remainder of the ban, I returned two positive breath tests for alcohol, on 5 May 2021 at Chester, and on 8 October 2021 at Newmarket. I received a ten-day ban for the first offence, and a 90-day ban for the second. Once again, during the investigations I attempted to deceive the people involved and my only excuse for doing so was that at the time my drinking was out of control. It was, as I said at the eventual hearing, the rock on which I perished.

My addiction to alcohol and the destruction that caused, not just to me but a lot of people who are close to me, and which has all been very well documented by the press and the media, is something that, with a great deal of help from the aforementioned people and others, I have fortunately been able to control so far and will hopefully continue doing so. It is a daily struggle. My addiction to what I do for a living, on the other hand – and it is a form of addiction in my opinion and is one that I'd say the majority of people who work with horses are afflicted by – is a different beast altogether. Being an alcoholic often involves drinking in order to remove yourself from reality, whereas my addiction to horses and horse racing is the opposite, in that it's the reality I crave more than anything else on God's earth. The alcohol helped me to cope with the parts of that reality that I did and still do find most challenging. There's an irony in there somewhere.

The question I was asked by various friends of mine immediately after agreeing to write this book was 'Why on earth are you doing it?' The assumption being, I think, that the life of a jockey is intensive and time-consuming enough without having to repeat it all again on paper. It was a fair enough question but was one I could easily answer. 'I see it as being a form of therapy,' I told those who asked. 'Therapy' being the first word that came into my head when I was approached about writing an account of my life in real time.

Since October 2021, I have been having counselling sessions twice a week and without these sessions I would be in a very different place to where I am now. They are extremely important to me and my hope when I started writing this book was that reliving the days just past might become an extension of that therapy. And has it? Well, I'm not going to tell you right now. I might do at the end of the book. There is a difference, though, so I've learned, between simply recalling an experience you have been through and reliving every moment in your head. Learning to practise the former and resisting the latter is a skill I've had to learn very quickly indeed during this process and is one that I wish I had acquired many, many years earlier.

With regards to at which point in time I should start the book, I eventually came to the conclusion that, as with my recovery from alcoholism, just getting on and doing it was the right way to go and so the book starts on the day that I made that very same decision. At this point in time I haven't decided when it'll finish yet, but the obsessive in me might keep it going forever. Either way, I very much hope you enjoy it.

ONE

Riding Out

Somewhere between Newmarket and Lambourn

ON THE FACE OF IT, deciding to begin a book – a book that is supposed to demonstrate in detail what it is like being a jockey – on day three of a seventeen-day suspension might not be the best idea I've ever had. Then again, suspensions are part and parcel of what we jockeys go through (me more than most over recent years) so I'm actually OK with it.

This morning I was up at the crack of dawn and have been over in Newmarket riding out for two trainers, George Boughey and James Ferguson. I'm now in my car driving back home to Lambourn which I'll wager is where many of these entries will be made from. I dread to think what percentage of my life I spend in cars either driving or being driven to or from racing yards or race meetings. Although it can get a bit monotonous sometimes it's often the only time I get to myself.

The current ban I'm serving is made up of three different

suspensions, one that was served to me in Qatar, one that was served to me a week later during the Saudi Cup meeting which I'll come on to in just a second, and then one that was served to me a week or so after that at Wolverhampton. I was actually in agreement with the first suspension in Qatar but thought the other two were quite harsh. The stewards' decisions are always final, of course, but it doesn't mean you have to agree with them, either publicly or privately. I didn't and still don't.

The Saudi Cup meeting first took place in 2020 but I made my first visit to Saudi Arabia in 2018 for a King's Cup meeting. I remember feeling quite nervous when I first arrived there. I'm not sure whether they were police or army, but there were an awful lot of heavily armed and serious-looking men knocking about the place and I felt very much like an outsider. Which I suppose I was. Over the last few years as the Saudi Cup meeting has grown in stature and people have got to know each other, things have improved immeasurably and when I go there now I feel very safe and relaxed. My girlfriend Lizzy came with me this year and we had a lovely time. The non-drinking culture obviously plays in my favour and the restaurants and hotels are superb.

Results-wise, things didn't go my way this year unfortunately. I finished third on Giavellotto, riding for trainer Marco Botti in the Longines Red Sea Turf Handicap, which was my best result of the meeting. A colt called The Foxes that I rode for Andrew Balding in the Howden Neom Turf Cup was probably the biggest disappointment. I was happy with the horse's build-up to the race and my position at the start, but for some reason he couldn't pick up the pressure and dropped away quite unexpectedly. It was a mystery to all concerned as to why that happened, but you cannot legislate for these things. The vast majority of people are sympathetic to this fact but you'll always get one or two who like to accuse the jockey of not trying. And what do they have in common? They'll all have lost money, that's what.

I went into the Saudi Cup meeting with a strike rate of 22 per cent since the start of the year (twenty wins from seventy-seven rides), which is roughly what I'll need to achieve later on if I'm to challenge for champion jockey. I'm a dreadful sleeper at the best of times and knowing that my strike rate has dropped can be lethal. It's one of many things that keep me awake at night but is also what helps me to sleep when I'm doing well. My general routine tends to compound the former. For instance, because I had such a busy day yesterday, I didn't get to bed until well after midnight and then I was up again this morning before six to ride out.

Introducing more night meetings has been detrimental in this regard as they often prevent jockeys from getting to bed at a decent hour. Not that that means very much to me at the moment. Sleep deprivation aside, as well as helping me to identify talented horses, riding out, which is the term used for exercising horses (also known as hacking), sets me up for the day and gives me a sense of purpose and achievement. Feeling lazy is worse than feeling tired in my book, so regardless of how much sleep I've had or haven't had, I just have to get on with it.

I had a counselling session yesterday morning and my therapist made the point, and not for the first time, that racing isn't everything and that I should try and take what I do for a living a little bit less seriously. The trouble is that my world is so small and I allow it to take over. I am trying to change my perspective on things but it isn't easy. In fact, at this very moment in time I'd say it feels just about impossible, such is the hold that racing and horses have over my life. Suspension? What suspension. OK, so I'm not able to race for seventeen days, but I am still immersed in the sport every minute of the day. It isn't always like this. Sometimes I can let go of things a bit and allow my mind to wander on to other things such as football and what's in the news. It never lasts very long but the fact that it happens at all offers me some crumbs of comfort.

My therapist also asked me if I ever discuss any of the above with my fellow jockeys, which I most certainly do not. It's not that we don't get on with one another, as most of us do. At the end of the day though we are in competition, and so discussing possible weaknesses would be counter-intuitive at best.

I often wonder what people think of me while I'm chatting to them. It's just a question that pops into my head sometimes. How you are perceived by others is an important part of being a jockey – to fellow jockeys, trainers, owners and even horses – and regardless of how I'm feeling when I arrive at the gallops to ride out or at a race meeting, I will always give off the air of being confident and in good humour. It can be incredibly difficult to maintain sometimes but it has to be done.

Anything that's said between us jockeys, either in or out of the weighing room, is almost always banter-related. Jokes at each other's expense are the usual line, but there's often a story going around about one of the younger contingent catching an STD or something. It might be light-hearted, but you miss it when it isn't there. Ask a jockey what they miss most when they retire and in many cases the weighing room will be right up there. When I got suspended for fourteen months I missed the banter of the weighing room as much as anything else. Racing can be a terribly serious business at the best of times, and the fact that any one of us could end up either dead or in a wheelchair is, while rarely spoken about, never far away. The weighing room injects the proceedings with some much-needed levity for us jockeys and creates an oasis of camaraderie within what is in fact a cauldron of competition and peril.

I could probably count on the fingers of one hand the number of serious conversations I've had with any of my fellow jockeys, although I do have an example of one that happened quite recently. The week before the Saudi meeting I was waiting at Doha Airport with Ryan Moore, Jim Crowley and William Buick (having all raced in Qatar), and we ended up having a four-hour discussion over dinner about the future of British racing. I don't want to say too much as the discussion was private, but we were all in agreement about the potentially detrimental effect the government eyeing the racing industry for extra revenue will have on prize money while bemoaning the fact that other jurisdictions such as Japan, Hong Kong and even the USA have much better systems in place.

Anyway, on to these suspensions of mine (all for careless riding), which on the first two occasions were for failing to stay straight out of the stalls.

The first one in Qatar was a three-day suspension and the second one in Saudi, which I got riding Matilda Picotte in the Saudi National Bank 1351 Turf Sprint, was a five-day suspension. I was drawn fourteenth in that race which was the widest of all, and as I pushed to get towards the inside, a rider behind me got a bit of interference which forced him to take a precautionary measure. In most countries a transgression like that would result in a two-day suspension at most or even a caution, so I was very disappointed.

Eight days after returning home from Saudi, I received a nine-day suspension for an incident at Wolverhampton that resulted in Joe Fanning coming out of the side door and being knocked unconscious. As we were approaching the finish line, he bounced off me twice, I bounced off him twice, and then he went flying. Joe bouncing off me was deemed to have been accidental whereas me bouncing off him was deemed to have been a result of careless riding, and so that was that. Because he became unseated, the minimum ban was seven days, but they gave me an extra two for good measure. Seventeen days total, though. We're only a few pages in and you must be thinking I'm an awfully dirty rider.

The headline in some of the papers after I picked up the ban at Wolverhampton was that I'd miss the start of the season, which isn't true. What they were referring to, and for the sake of creating a headline, I think, is the old Flat season that ran from the Doncaster meeting in March to the Doncaster meeting in November. The season that's been in place ever since I've been a professional jockey runs from Guineas weekend at Newmarket at the beginning of May to British Champions Day at Ascot on the third Saturday in October. It looks like quite a short season on paper, but when you're stuck in the middle of it, believe me it's plenty long enough.

You might be wondering what a jockey gets up to while they're serving a ban. For me personally, I tend to go into overdrive. This week, for instance, I've ridden out for Owen

Burrows and Sir Mark Todd, I've been to Kempton to ride out for David Menuisier, I've been to Newmarket this morning to ride one for George Boughey and one for James Ferguson, I'll go to Andrew Balding's tomorrow to ride five or six, and then next week I'll ride out for Joseph O'Brien in Ireland as well as for lots of small trainers whom you've probably never heard of.

The reason I do this is to try and identify horses that I can win on in the future. Two-year-olds who are unraced and have their whole futures ahead of them. It's a numbers game, obviously, and if I don't put the hours in and help to find the talent, you can guarantee that somebody else will. One thing's for sure, there will be no downtime whatsoever during the ban. That's the safest bet of all.

One thing I stop doing quite so much while I'm serving a ban is monitoring my weight, the irony being that because I've got so much going on, it tends not to fluctuate too much. At this very moment in time I'm still under 9 stone which is very good for me.

Another erroneous headline that's been doing the rounds just recently is that I've been riding out regularly for Aidan O'Brien and according to one of the papers am apparently 'in pole position to pick up some big rides for the all-conquering O'Brien family'. The truth of the matter is that before I moved to England, I used to work full-time for Aidan and I've been riding out for him on a casual basis for donkey's years. Our arrangement hasn't changed at all, in that I will continue riding out for Aidan as and when he asks me to, but I will not be moving to Ireland. I also 'pick up' rides for Aidan's sons sometimes, a notable example being a Group 1 win I had for Donnacha O'Brien at the back end of last year. Donnacha also has a very promising filly called Porta Fortuna that I've ridden a few times and should run in the Guineas trial in April. Anyway, with regards to the headline, it must have been a slow news day or something.

Talking of journalists, I was asked by one the other day what I was looking forward to about the Classics this year and I had to answer, not very much at all. Things can obviously change, but at this very moment in time I don't have a confirmed ride for any of them. The only light at the end of the tunnel regarding the Derby at the moment is one of David Menuisier's horses called Sunway. I won a Group 1 on him in France at the end of last year and he's been bred to stay. Before he even raced I remember telling Sheikh Fahad, who is the chairman of Qatar Racing and one of my main employers, what a good horse I thought he was. Then, after he won first time out at Sandown, Sheikh Fahad managed to buy a piece of him, which was good. He might end up being a Derby horse, although when I won on him last year I didn't think he'd be a very strong stayer over twelve furlongs. Before we get there, I have got nothing definite for the Guineas at the moment, which is a worry. Anyway, we carry on.

Incidentally, I've now made the decision to go for champion jockey this year. I'd been in two minds for a while now. After all, the workload and mental strain involved in going for the championship are off the scale, and once you decide to go for it, it occupies every minute of your day while you're awake and sometimes while you're asleep. You don't take any days off (unless you're suspended) and even if you find yourself in a social situation, all you'll be thinking about is where the next win is coming from. For six whole months it owns every single bit of you.

Somebody asked me a couple of years ago why jockeys who aren't necessarily going to win the championship carry on pushing themselves to that level.

'What's the motivation to keep on chasing?' he said.

Put very simply, the more winners you ride as a jockey, the more opportunities you'll have to ride better horses which in turn will improve your chances of winning the championship. A good example would be young Billy Loughnane. His work ethic over the past couple of years has been incredible and sooner or later he'll be far enough up the ladder to be able to go for the big one.

Only time will tell if I've made the right decision by going for it again. I'll be putting a heck of a lot on the line, that's for sure. Not least my sanity, such as it is.

FRIDAY, 22 MARCH 2024

Lambourn

I was asked yesterday how I first became interested in horses. It's probably one of the most popular questions jockeys are asked, so I thought I would cover it here if that's OK.

I don't remember any of this, but according to my mother I was exposed to horses from a very young age. Her father, my grandad, absolutely adored racing and on a Saturday afternoon I'd sit on his lap and watch it with him. He'd pretend to ride the final furlong of every race with me as the jockey and apparently I loved it. My uncle is the former jump jockey Jim Culloty, and my mother said when he was on the TV, my grandad used to become very animated. Once again, I must have had no idea what was going on, but over time I started to become quite enamoured with it all. The drama, the noise, the colours and, of course, the horses.

There was a small racing yard about two miles from where we lived in County Kerry that belonged to a man called Charlie Coakley. Mr Coakley can't have had more than about ten horses, and when I was three years old my mother took me there one day and I was put on a horse and led around the yard.

Having been born eleven weeks premature and weighing about the same as a bag of sugar, I'd matured a bit slower than my contemporaries and had had to have some serious interventions as a baby. It was something to do with my bone development not being what it should have been and I had to have a lot of occupational therapy. Be that as it may, according to my parents I never let it hold me back and came away from Mr Coakley's yard absolutely full of it. 'Can I have riding lessons? Can I? Can I? Can I?' It was full on pester power.

I must have worn them down eventually as on my fourth birthday on 6 September 1999, my father's sister Rosie took me to a riding school in Milltown, County Kerry called Abbeyglen Equestrian, which is still going strong. I'm afraid I don't remember any of the lessons (which is undoubtedly down to my poor memory as opposed to the quality of instruction), but when I was seven years of age my father decided to buy me a pony. He was called Rusty due to his colour but I couldn't pronounce my Rs so used to say Wusty. Looking back, Rusty was probably one of the most ill-mannered animals I have ever had to ride and he took almost as much pleasure bucking me off as I did getting back on again. I was still extremely small for my age and he knew I was weak. Gradually though, I managed to build my strength up and took control. A bit.

Although my first introduction to horses as a spectator was racing, it was showjumping that pulled me in. By the time I was nine I had a couple of ponies and had regular lessons with some really good people. A bit later on my Uncle Don bought me a three-year-old pony. When he turned four, I began competing with him and I eventually won a Discovery Class at Millstreet in County Cork. That was the first thing I ever won on a horse.

Slowly but surely the number of ponies I had in my care grew, and by the time I was fourteen I had upwards of ten. It all sounds very grand but it was partly self-funded as I used to buy and sell them. It was about this time that I started racing ponies which was a precursor to becoming a jockey. My Uncle Jim used to very kindly lend us his horse lorry sometimes which would enable us to take seven or eight ponies to a show. My sisters used to help out with tacking and the warming up and we had quite a bit of success. Even at that age I appreciated how incredibly privileged I was to be able to do something like that and I attempted to repay my parents' faith and investment by always doing my best and by taking it very seriously. In fact, I used to put myself under a huge amount of pressure to deliver in competitions but this was offset by the amount of enjoyment I would get from them.

This week I've been flat out riding two-year-olds that are going to the breeze-up sales. From Monday to Thursday I rode out no fewer than sixty-four of these horses, for a number of different consignors, and loved every solitary moment. The quality of the horses varied, of course, but I've been like a child in a sweet shop all week.

For those of you who might not be aware, breeze-up sales are when unraced two-year-olds are worked in a gallop over two furlongs which allows potential buyers to get a good view of which horses they might or might not wish to buy. The majority of these horses will have been bought as yearlings by their consignors who spend the next six months breaking them in and getting them ready to gallop. My role is to identify horses that I believe have a future and then notify Sheikh Fahad at Qatar Racing who may or may not decide to buy them.

The concept of the breeze-up sale originated in America about fifty years ago and back then involved nothing more than horses being saddled up and cantered up the straight. It's evolved a bit since then but not much.

One of the most exciting aspects of this process for me is getting to ride horses that are by stallions that I either raced against or rode myself. The pick of the horses I rode this week was by a horse called Kameko ('by' refers to the sire and 'out of' means the dam), whom I won on many times for Andrew Balding, and the dam (mother) is a horse that David Simcock used to train called Miss Sugars. There were also a few by an excellent horse called Earthlight this time around, which is owned by Godolphin. In total I'd say there were probably six or seven that in my opinion could go on to become decent racehorses. The others felt quite ordinary at the moment, but that can change.

While I'm here it might be helpful to write a few words about how commercial breeding actually works.

Covering fees for a stallion range from £5,000 to £350,000

and the best mares obviously go to the best stallions. Most stallions will cover from one hundred to two hundred mares a year and there's an art (or some would say a science) to deciding which mare should be sent to which stallion.

Breeders such as Juddmonte and Godolphin need to decide which brood mares should be kept and which should be sold on. Get it wrong, which they sometimes do, and it can cost you a fortune. Or make somebody else a fortune, depending on which side of the deal you're on.

Another example of how precarious the business can be is how fragile, or unlucky, the progeny are. For instance, if a foal comes out alive and is by a prominent stallion like Frankel or Dubawi, as a breeder you will have paid £350,000 for that result. If, heaven forbid, that foal then breaks a leg the following day, you have no comeback.

Anyway, that's it in a nutshell.

Another reason why I've been feeling quite up this week is because the pressure of racing has been off. It's the last week of my ban and I've been in a great mood. Then again, the workload has been just as hectic. There's been an awful lot of travelling and my schedule's been insane. The kick I get out of riding those horses though. It's just incredible. What adds to the excitement is that I'm not afraid to put my money on the line and buy some of these horses myself if I think they're good enough (and if Sheikh Fahad doesn't buy them), with the idea of selling them on.

Buying and selling horses is something I've dabbled in since I was a teenager (in that case it was ponies) and as well as thoroughly enjoying it I've got a decent track record. The last horse of note that I bought was Dragon Symbol whom I sent to Archie Watson and eventually sold to a Japanese owner. He cost me £150,000 and turned out to be a very good horse. He'll be popping up later, I should imagine, when I talk about Royal Ascot.

I should have seen this coming really, but when I told my therapist about my love of buying and selling horses, she immediately said, 'Then why don't you make it your profession?' It was as though she'd struck gold or something. Anything but being an actual jockey! 'But as soon as I make it my profession the fun would disappear,' I argued. She looked disappointed.

One of the reasons I love buying and selling horses is because I don't have to worry about it or rely on it for anything. It's purely about the enjoyment and is how I like to gamble, I suppose. Also, the horses I'm asked to ride will be the best on the market, yet the moment I made it my profession I'd have to ride and consider everything out there. What at the moment is something very special to me would immediately become very ordinary. Ordinary horses in ordinary circumstances. I couldn't do that. Well, I could, I suppose. But I wouldn't want to.

Another reason why I could never do it for a living is because it's pretty tight economically and the men and women who do it professionally put themselves under a severe amount of pressure. Some do very well out of it, but all it takes is a run of bad luck and the odd bad decision and you're well and truly in the mire.

Let's say you go to the yearling sales in October and lay out two million quid for twenty yearlings, which wouldn't be out of the ordinary. All of a sudden it's mid-March and the breeze-up sales are from the first week in April until the end of May. It's hard to get horses into these sales at the best of times, but what if some of these yearlings have sore shins, a cough or even ringworm which can spread. All of a sudden your opportunity has gone which means you'll have to race them yourself (yet more expense) as it's almost impossible to sell a horse from just a workout on a gallop. You are allowed to sell horses outside the sales (as long as you don't take the Mickey) but unless you're like the ex-jockey Norman Williamson who has a regular list of clients, you've got no chance.

For all the pressure and potential pitfalls, the fact that I race horses at quite a high level means I don't have to worry about money day to day, whereas these guys very often do. A lot of people say to me that they could never cope with what I do for a living but understand why I do it. It's the same for me with people who trade horses. I get it, but I couldn't do it. Not all the time.

So, what have I been up to today and what do I have planned for the weekend and next week? This morning I was at Ollie Sangster's, who is the grandson of legendary breeder and owner Robert Sangster. Ollie started training last year and I won a Listed race and came second in a Group 2 on a filly he trains called Shuwari, whom he also owns a piece of. Ollie received some terrible news a few days ago that Shuwari has fractured her pelvis which means she'll miss the 1,000 Guineas. There was talk of her being my ride in the Guineas a while ago, but I'd had to give her up as Porta Fortuna, See The Fire and the French champion filly, Ramatuelle, are all heading towards that race. Ollie's gutted about the horse, as am I. He's doing a great job though and this morning I rode a Kingman filly for him out of Farmah, who I think will win first time out. Ollie will be a top trainer in a few years, I'm quite sure of that.

Incidentally, choosing which horses to ride can often be a complicated business. It's down to connections usually and I have to weigh up how a decision will affect me both now and in the future. There have been several occasions when I've decided to turn down chances of winning Group 1 races in order to get more opportunities going forward. It's not an exact science, as they say. More's the pity.

Tomorrow I'm at Andrew Balding's where I'll probably ride out six or seven horses and then on Sunday I'm going back to Ireland to ride more breeze-up horses for a variety of trainers on the Monday. As much as I've been enjoying these past two weeks, I must admit that I'm absolutely exhausted. Depending on where I've been travelling to or from, I've been getting up as early as half past four in the morning and have been arriving home, or wherever I've been staying at the time, well after dark most days. I'm probably running on adrenaline at the moment so I'll have to be careful. Not just physically, but mentally too. The racing resumes next week and because I've been on such a high just recently, I might be in for a decline, especially if I'm having to waste, which I will be. That's what usually happens.

One of the most memorable declines I've had took place some time in 2018. I'd had six or seven rides a day all over the country for something like eight days on the spin with loads of winners. I was flying. The following day I flew to Leopardstown to ride one for Willie Mullins, after which I took a plane back to Oxford and got to bed about midnight. After managing to snatch three hours' sleep, I got up to fly to Canada the next morning where I spent approximately five hours to ride in one race before travelling straight back to England. My head hit my pillow at about midnight and the following day I was up at the crack to ride out and then had six rides at somewhere like Kempton. When I finally got back home, I barely knew where I was. I had nothing left. No energy, no enthusiasm. Not even adrenaline. I was spent, both physically and mentally.

The reason I remember this episode is because ironically, I *don't* remember it. At least the detail. I don't remember any of the rides and I barely even remember travelling to Canada. What I do remember is sitting at home at the end of it all feeling dead.

Funnily enough, I have been thinking about when I might get a chance to recharge my batteries a bit and as daft as it might sound, one of the most obvious opportunities will be the plane journey both to and from the Dubai World Cup. I'm at Newcastle next Friday evening, after which I'll take a small plane down to Denham Airfield in Buckinghamshire and then catch an overnight flight from Heathrow to Dubai. I'm fairly sure I land at about 8.45 in the morning and don't have a ride until 12.40pm. This will give me a couple more hours to relax in my hotel room.

It probably sounds ridiculous me planning to recuperate on a red-eye flight and then in a hotel room for a few hours before one of the most prestigious race meetings of the year, but to me it makes perfect sense. On a plane there are no distractions at all – horses, trainers, owners, family, friends, agents, press – which means I can completely switch off. It's bliss.

I've been hovering around the 9-stone mark this week which isn't bad at all. I have 8st 7lb to make by Wednesday for Andrew on a horse called Juantorena, although there is a chance that the weights might go up by two pounds to 8st 9lb.

This might be a good time to explain the handicap system, for those who don't know. Put very simply, horses are weighted according to a rating that is meant to represent their form and perceived ability at any given time. A better horse will carry a heavier weight and a lesser horse will obviously carry a lighter one. Younger horses will also get an allowance against older horses which offsets the disparity in size and maturity. The ratings are allocated by the BHA and weights rise in races if the horses at the top of the handicap don't run or declare. That's for the UK and Ireland, by the way. It's different in other countries.

This morning I was 9 stone exactly and I looked light in the face. I've been grafting hard and haven't been eating much at all. If my weight doesn't come down naturally though in the next couple of days, I'll have a fair bit of torture ahead of me on Monday and Tuesday. Then again, if I had to I could probably lose half a stone between now and tomorrow morning so it isn't that much of an issue. It stresses me, the weight thing, but it very rarely panics me.

As wasting is such a big part of our lives, it probably deserves a few paragraphs in isolation. Not that you'll find a jockey anywhere on earth who takes pleasure from talking or writing about it, least of all doing it. It's the proverbial necessary evil for us and is never, ever pleasurable. In fact, if you had to measure how the experience varies, you might say that it comes in varying degrees of shit. I hate it. We all hate it. But the majority of us have to do it.

Some people assume, understandably perhaps, that wasting is something that gets harder as you get older, but in my experience that isn't the case. When I started out as a jockey I found wasting incredibly difficult because I wasn't used to having to lose weight. During my entire career in pony racing I never had to lose more than a pound or two at a time and so it was never an issue.

Fast-forward to my first few rides as a working apprentice jockey and I had what you might call a bit of a rude awakening. I had five or six pounds to lose quickly and it completely knocked me for six. I knew nothing about things such as salt tablets and got terrible cramps from the dehydration. It was agonizing.

Because I wasn't very well versed on weight management in those days I used to fill up on electrolytes and fizzy drinks straight after a meeting and would wake up the next day even heavier. This turned into a kind of yo-yo cycle for me and I became addicted to both. I couldn't resist them. I've become a lot more disciplined these days but I still get cravings on a regular basis.

I've been aware of wasting for as long as I can remember. My Uncle Jim used to come back to Ireland from England at Christmas sometimes and I never remember him eating very much. It must have been torture for him being around so much food and drink. I also remember my grandad telling me stories about Jim's mood during the Galway Festival. He always had light weights and according to Grandad, Jim could be a bit of a grouch sometimes. Understandably! I also remember weighing myself a lot in my teens so it was definitely on my radar as something to watch out for. As I said though, before becoming a jockey it wasn't a problem for me as I never had much to lose.

How you manage wasting day to day will obviously dictate how painful it is. I've been checking my weight on a regular basis since I was a teenager but never to such an extent as it's become an obsession. You might find that strange coming from someone like me – i.e. an obsessive – but I'm aware that by weighing myself five times a day and obsessing about it, which some jockeys do, I'll be jeopardizing my performance in the saddle and therefore my chances of winning.

Last year I had a few days off over Christmas and was due to ride in Florida on 29 December. I thought I'd kept on top of my weight quite well during that time but when I got on the scales over there for the first time I was 9st 2lb so 58 kilos. In just thirty-six hours I had to be 8st 6lb so had to lose ten pounds. Not to put too fine a point on it, the process of achieving this was torture. I promise you, it was horrific. I got in a sweatsuit and did three ninety-minute sessions in the gym between the treadmill, the rower and the bike, I did two two-hour stints in the bath at a constant temperature of 40 degrees, I jogged from my apartment to the racecourse in a sweatsuit and then I jumped straight in the sauna when I got there. I ended up making the weight but only just. God, I felt awful.

Some unusually tall jockeys such as Adam Kirby and George Baker, who are five foot eleven and six foot respectively, would have had to do this all the time. It just doesn't bear thinking about. Even guys who manage their weight successfully such as Ryan Moore will occasionally have a mountain to climb, especially when riding in America. The best horses often carry light weights and if you want to ride them you have no choice.

Having to waste is one of the things that forces jockeys into early retirement, especially if you've been successful. One day you just wake up and think, *Why am I putting my body through this?* It doesn't matter how good your diet is, what you're doing to yourself is unnatural.

I never feel like I can eat like a normal person. The parameters we have to work within are minuscule in comparison and whereas a man of my height and build (I'm five foot six) might consume two and a half thousand calories in a day (which is the average) and think nothing of it, I would go into meltdown, not just mentally but physically. I probably consume an average of twelve hundred calories a day so consuming over double that would be a huge shock to my system. That twelve hundred calories consists mainly of things like porridge, if I can have it, boiled eggs, a little bit of fruit at the track, a Haribo or two (other sweeties are available), and if I'm feeling a bit flat a coffee or an energy drink. In the evening I'll try and have something that doesn't simply remind me that I'm starving myself, such as chicken or fish.

With regards to safety, there are more factors with wasting than simply what you put into your body. Or should I say, what you don't put into your body. For instance, the British Horseracing Authority, the BHA, in their infinite wisdom, closed the saunas at racecourses permanently after Covid which has resulted in dozens of jockeys now driving to meetings wearing sweatsuits with the heating in their cars turned fully on. That was all done, as they reiterated in a statement in August 2023, because they are 'committed to the safety, welfare and mental wellbeing of racing's participants'. What, by forcing them to sweat in their cars while they're on their way to a meeting? That's just ridiculous.

I went to a meeting at York last year at which the BHA claimed that racecourses couldn't get insurance for jockeys sweating in saunas. I don't believe that for a second. Since I've been riding in Britain I have never heard of one incident of a jockey having a health issue either during or after taking a sauna at a racecourse. The Professional Jockeys Association could challenge this madness but unfortunately they have neither the will nor the strength necessary to do so. Or so it would appear.

Anyway, rant over. At least for now.

29 MARCH 2024 – GOOD FRIDAY

A1 south of Newcastle

Today went from being quite a good day to being a disaster. Well, not a disaster exactly, but a day that I'm keen to forget. I picked up a six-day suspension for one strike too many on a horse called Vaguely Royal in the Good Friday Marathon at Newcastle. I was finishing the race in fifth and had no chance. It was a genuine mistake.

The maximum amount of times you're allowed to use a whip for encouragement during a Flat race is six times in Britain, four in France and seven in Ireland. The penalty structure is incredibly severe. If you go one over in the UK, for instance, the penalty ranges from two days to eight days. For one misdemeanour.

As the race in Newcastle was worth £150k total prize money, my suspension should have been eight days, but because I'd not been suspended for a whip breach in over two hundred rides, it was reduced to six. Had I committed the same breach in the Listed Burradon Stakes on the same card, in which I finished a narrowly beaten second, I would be facing a two-day ban. I'm trying to make the point that this doesn't make any sense as diplomatically as possible but to be honest with you, I'm furious. Furious and frustrated.

This means that I will now miss the entire Craven Meeting at Newmarket. I'm in danger of sounding like I'm feeling sorry for myself but I'm properly fed up. I mean, why can't they just fine us? Hit us in the pocket. As I said, I was finishing fifth on Vaguely Royal and had no chance of being placed, so why would I go one over. It was a genuine mistake. A genuine mistake that could now have a material effect on my year. If a footballer receives a yellow or red card that they believe to be unjust, they have leave to appeal. We don't for whip bans. I'm really not happy at the moment.

While we're on the subject of the whip, as it's such a contentious issue both at and away from the track, I thought it might be of interest to let you know where I stand on its use in horse racing.

It probably won't surprise you to learn that I'm very pro retaining the whip in British racing and don't feel its removal would have the positive effect that some people claim it would. In fact, I think the opposite would be true. As with racing itself, the kind of people who are advocating against jockeys using the whip are the same or similar people who wrongly believe that racehorses are all poorly treated and are in pain all the time. The sport isn't perfect by any means and there will still be instances when horses aren't treated as well as they should be. It is policed rigorously, though, and those who are found guilty of mistreating horses are rightly punished.

In some jurisdictions such as Germany, because the strokes are so limited (a jockey can use the whip just three times during the entire race), the jockeys aren't in harmony with the horses as much. They have to rely more on bouncing up and down and shaking the reins at them. This is obviously even worse in countries such as Norway and Sweden where the whip has been banned altogether.

If a jockey isn't allowed to use the stick for encouragement during a race, it's very hard to know for sure whether a horse has run to the best of its ability, regardless of how many times you shake the reins or jump up and down. If I hit myself down the side of my leg with a jockey's stick it isn't going to hurt. I've tried it and it doesn't. They're light, are padded with foam and absorb energy. As importantly, they no longer have the loop of leather at the end.

These days, whips are all about noise rather than impact and we use them to startle a horse and make them more alert and responsive if anything. Most people don't realize this which is a problem in itself. The vast majority of jockeys would never go out of their way to hurt a horse, and if they did, they wouldn't last two minutes.

When the new design of whip was first introduced, a journalist from the *Guardian* newspaper visited the jockey Jim Crowley to discuss it. In order to demonstrate the difference between this and the old type of whip, Jim suggested hitting the journalist over the palm of his hand (which is one of the most sensitive parts of the body) with the same amount of force as he'd hit a horse during a race. The journalist bravely agreed to Jim's suggestion and guess what, he barely felt a thing.

I know that various associations keep on coming up with studies suggesting that horses might feel pain when we use the whip or that whips don't work for encouragement, but if you look for something hard enough, regardless of how tenuous it is, the chances are you'll find a speck of it somewhere.

None of these people have ever asked me for my opinion on this or about my experiences. Probably because I might not give them the answers they're looking for.

About three years ago, the BHA was forced to make a U-turn after it banned jockeys from using the whip in a forehand position. This was one of the few occasions when our collective displeasure made a difference and the BHA replaced the ban with an amendment to the rules that resulted in what we have now: that the whip can be used six times in a Flat race and seven times in a jumps race, which was down from seven and eight respectively.

I actually view the use of the whip as an art form in some cases. Especially when you watch protagonists such as Frankie Dettori or Andrea Atzeni. The way they pull the stick through from one side to the other and switch from backhand to forehand is amazing. They have such balance and rhythm. It's a beautiful thing to watch.

In countries where use of the whip for encouragement has been banned completely, racing is in decline. Why? Well, racing is funded mainly by betting and a percentage of the money that the betting companies make goes back into the sport for things like prize money and infrastructure at the racecourses. A punter will only bet on a horse if he or she believes that it is being encouraged to run well. If they don't, they'll bet on a horse that's running somewhere else and is being encouraged, hence the massive decline in places like Scandinavia. It's a pity because twenty or thirty years ago racing was thriving over there.

Ironically, as far as horse welfare is concerned, this could create a huge dilemma. As horse racing slowly goes to the wall, some of the horses might be re-employed, but the majority won't. And who's going to pay for their upkeep? Thousands of them might have to be euthanized.

Despite what I've written above, I'm actually in favour of many of the changes that have been introduced regarding the whip over the years (especially the introduction of the foam whip), and the fact that its use continues to be policed, monitored and modified when necessary is right and correct. What I don't have any time or respect for is the ongoing campaign by certain groups to bully and embarrass racing authorities into banning the whip altogether. It's the kind of virtue signalling we can well do without in racing and it's important that the BHA stand firm.

TWO

The Circuit

TUESDAY, 2 APRIL 2024

Lambourn

I WOKE UP THIS MORNING to the tragic news that the jockey Stefano Cherchi has passed away. He had a fall at Canberra Racetrack last month and unfortunately he never recovered from his injuries. He was only twenty-three years old and I'd known him since he was a teenager. Like me, Frankie Dettori and so many other foreign jockeys, Stefano had left his home country when he was just a lad, full of nerves and hope, his only real possession being an inalienable dream of riding the best horses in the biggest races on the planet. It's so sad.

He'd been riding for Amy Murphy in Newmarket for the last couple of years and then after riding in Australia over the winter he decided to relocate there. Stefano used to text me and ask me for advice sometimes, which I was always happy to give. I've been looking through some of our conversations on my phone. He was always so polite and so grateful. An absolute gent. The entire racing world will be in mourning today, that's for sure. I'll be saying a prayer for his family later.

Stefano's death is yet another stark reminder of how dangerous horse racing can be. It's by far the most dangerous major sport on earth with an average of two jockeys a year losing their lives and a further sixty being left paralysed. Suicide is also becoming a huge issue in the jockey community but that's for another day.

Riding thoroughbreds at 40mph in a competitive environment is always going to be dangerous, yet here we all are. For every 1,000 jockeys, 606 will get injured in any one year. That's a disquieting statistic whichever way you look at it. It can all end in a flash. Not that you ever leave the weighing room before a race thinking that this might be either your last race or your final few minutes on earth. If it was it would drive you around the bend. I have spent a lot of time thinking about it over the years and I'm aware of my own mortality. I'm also a realist and at the end of the day it's part of the job.

I don't want to get too maudlin here, but I have been looking at sorting out a living will for myself just recently which is a kind of advanced healthcare directive. If, for instance, I had a fall and suffered a serious brain injury, I would not want to live and would hope that whoever was in charge of my care would adhere to my wishes and find some way of letting me go. It isn't the kind of thing you can discuss with your family very easily so I decided to go down the legal route instead. It's a contentious subject, I appreciate that, and I'm only twenty-eight years old. I'm just trying to do the right thing.

On a more cheery note, I did indeed manage to get some much-needed rest and relaxation during both legs of my journey to and from Dubai. I wouldn't say it recharged my batteries completely, but it was enjoyable. As I intimated earlier, it isn't necessarily the sleep that allows me to recuperate (which normally isn't the best on a plane), it's the environment I'm in.

On to the meeting.

My ride in the Dubai Gold Cup, Coltrane, was disappointing to say the least. He's an older horse and this was his first trip abroad which might have been a factor. The ground was also a bit fast for him, I think. There was always a fear that he might not perform to the best of his ability but unfortunately he exceeded that fivefold. The *Racing Post* summed up his race in two words – always behind.

The Gold Cup was the second of ten races on the day's card and with no more rides ahead of me I was able to switch off and become a racegoer for a change. It doesn't happen very often but when it does I can usually enjoy myself, especially watching such good horses.

Towards the end of the Dubai Turf, which was the 3.10, Christophe Lemaire's mount Catnip stumbled and was fatally injured. Christophe himself sustained a number of injuries including a punctured lung, a broken collarbone and a broken rib. He was rushed to hospital but was declared OK soon after, thank heavens.

Shortly before the start of the following race, I was approached by the trainer of Christophe's mount in the World Cup, a fellow called Hidetaka Otonashi. With the help of my Japanese interpreter, Hiroshi Ando, he asked me if I might be willing to step into the breach and cover for

Christophe, which I was obviously happy to do. I then went straight to the weighing room and watched some replays of the horse, called Derma Sotogake, in action. I'd never ridden him before but was aware of him as he won the UAE Derby at the same meeting last year.

It's funny what life can throw at you sometimes. One minute I'm a spectator just relaxing in the stands with some associates and the next minute I'm preparing to ride a fancied horse in the second richest horse race on earth. To be fair it wasn't too fantastical. Being asked to step in at the last minute for a jockey can happen often and for a variety of different reasons. Traffic, illness. It's not so much of a rarity.

As if almost sensing that something was awry, Derma Sotogake became fractious in the stalls and got quite worked up. He did well early on but we were squeezed out after a furlong and unfortunately he never recovered. He really wasn't happy at all and ended up finishing sixth. I've been beaten on a nose in the World Cup before (by a horse called Gronkowski, named after an NFL player) and had thought this might be my chance, but alas it wasn't to be. In hindsight though, I'm also glad he didn't win for Christophe's sake. I didn't get my hopes up too much (I didn't really have time to) so there was no harm done. The main thing is that Christophe is on the mend.

The closest I've come to missing such a prestigious race myself through injury was back in 2021. I was booked to ride a Japanese contender in the Prix de l'Arc de Triomphe called Chrono Genesis. She was second or third favourite for the race and when I'd ridden her a few weeks before she felt brilliant. I genuinely thought we had a very good chance of winning and I was pretty excited.

On the Thursday before the race I was down at Salisbury when disaster struck. I was about to ride a two-year-old called Oasis Gift belonging to Jeff Smith but as Andrew Balding gave me a leg-up in the parade ring, the horse bolted before jamming on the brakes in front of a railing. Normally a horse wouldn't have the capability to go from such a speed to an absolute standstill and especially on a surface where there isn't much grip. Unfortunately for me, Oasis Gift showed a talent for just that and my head went through a metal mesh railing ripping from just below my nose all the way down to my lip. The scar's not as obvious now but that's only thanks to me having had two rounds of plastic surgery. The fact that I wasn't concussed, which would have prevented me from travelling to Longchamp, not to mention riding in some big races at Newmarket the following day, was an absolute miracle, as was me not sustaining any other injuries such as a broken collarbone. As it turned out, Chrono Genesis didn't perform in the Arc, but I did manage to win a Group 1 for André Fabre on a horse named Zellie. You win some, you lose some.

MONDAY, 8 APRIL 2024

Lambourn

I had a day in France yesterday racing at Deauville. I left the house at 6am and didn't get home until gone 11pm, then I was up again at 5am this morning. So far today I've ridden out for Andrew Balding and Richard Hughes and to be honest I'm still feeling the effects of yesterday. I'm exhausted. It's fine when they run well and you have a couple of winners. It energizes you. But when they run a touch disappointingly and nothing goes your way, which is what happened yesterday, it's a long journey home. A win tends to compensate for the lack of energy, whereas if you lose, that and a feeling of disappointment is all you're left with. I tend to spend most of that time pondering what went wrong which definitely isn't healthy for someone like me.

In this case it could have been a number of things. For a start, thanks to Brexit, what was once a seamless formality getting horses through customs and into Europe has become a production with all the paperwork and I was told after my second race at Deauville that the two horses I rode – a colt called Devil's Point and a filly called Tamfana (both for David Menuisier) – had been stuck there for almost five hours. That's shameful really. Being Irish I thought I'd be exempt from the effects of Brexit but I was obviously wrong.

The ground was also very slow at Deauville which didn't suit Devil's Point at all. A fast ground horse such as him has to work so much harder on soft ground which affects their attitude as well as their performance. The ground issue can be overplayed sometimes but not in this case. Some horses genuinely want and need fast ground, and two furlongs out he just hit a wall and that was it. Tamfana, on the other hand, relishes that sort of surface and was very comfortable. It just wasn't her day unfortunately. On super-fast tracks such as Goodwood, even horses that enjoy fast ground can struggle with the pace sometimes. They get to the business end and then just give up. The trainer will always try and give you an idea of what to expect from a horse, but if it isn't really coping with the conditions, whether that be distance, ground or they're simply having an off day, it's your job as a jockey to protect the horse and look after them. My first concern is and always will be the horse.

Generally I've been very up and down these last few days. I've ridden a few winners (although not at Deauville) as well as one or two promising horses in the morning which has energized me. That's a word I probably overuse but it's genuinely how I feel when this happens. Feeling like that enables me to carry on with life's challenges day to day.

Speaking of which.

This morning I received an email from the Italian Racing Authority saying that they're going to fine me €5,000. According to them I went one over with the whip during a race over there in 2020. I say according to them because there was no stewards' enquiry after the race and I was never even informed. The only reason I thought there might be an issue is because they'd been withholding the prize money. The Italian Racing Authority are notoriously slow payers which has been their undoing in recent times, but four years is a bit much even for them.

It's hard to put into words just how ridiculous this situation is. Not to have a stewards' enquiry is bad enough but to let it go on for four years. Really? It's like the Premier League turning around to a team and docking them points for a goal that should have been disallowed four years ago, but without offering any kind of proof whatsoever. Unfortunately, unlike a Premier League football team that would undoubtedly challenge such a ridiculous decision and no doubt win, I just have to suck it up. What I can do, however, is exercise my right not to race in Italy ever again, which is probably what I'll do. It's nonsensical.

TUESDAY, 16 APRIL 2024

Lambourn

I've been serving that six-day suspension I got at Newcastle this past week. Fortunately, I haven't missed very much, although a horse I was booked to ride did win in Qatar last night. Missing winners is obviously not a good thing, although I was happy that Dan Muscutt was offered the ride instead as he's a friend of mine. It was a small field and I thought he had a good ride. Hopefully the horse won't be punished too much by the handicapper, who assesses each performance and rates a horse accordingly, and can win a few more. If he can't he's the right type of horse, having won over six and seven furlongs, to be trained in Hong Kong later on, as the resale market over there for horses that race between six furlongs and a mile and a quarter is massive. His future will be secure providing he stays healthy. If he does his next race will probably be on the turf in early to mid-May. You find that a lot of the three-year-old races this time of year are really competitive, but as we push forward a few weeks, once the majority have had their first outing, it'll be a lot easier to separate the wheat from the chaff.

I have two big days coming up at Newbury later this week which in some respects I'm looking forward to, but in others not. What's spoiling it for me is that the more I look at the programme book and the schedule of races, the more I end up asking myself why some of the horses I'm booked to ride haven't been entered in certain races.

This is a frustration I've had on numerous occasions over the years but you have to be very careful how you approach it. Telling or even suggesting to a racehorse trainer which races they should enter their horses in is literally telling them how to do their job. Even when you've ridden the horse previously you have to know whom you can talk to and when. For instance, I wouldn't dare have such a conversation with Andrew Balding or Sir Michael Stoute. Not because they aren't open to fresh ideas, but because they're at the very top of their game and telling someone of their stature and experience how to operate would be at best an impertinence and at worst a downright insult. Also, just because I think a horse should be entered in a certain race doesn't mean it would be the right decision. I still feel the frustration though, keenly, which has more to do with my passion for the sport than it does anything else. Yet again, I'd be advised not to take it so seriously by most people, but that option isn't on the cards. Some of the younger trainers such as James Ferguson, Ollie Sangster and Harry Charlton allow me to scratch the itch from time to time by involving me in such decisions, which I have to say helps. After Newbury I'll probably be less sensitized to it and less tense, but at the moment it's playing on my mind a lot.

I was going to change the subject here but the more I think about it – which is what I shouldn't be doing really as it's bad for me – the more it starts to make sense. There are very few jockeys on earth who are as forensic in their approach to what we do as I am, hence the frustration. Nor are there many who ride out as much as I do. I'll give you an example.

Tomorrow morning I'm riding out for Saeed bin Suroor, John Gosden, Sir Michael Stoute and Michael Bell and it'll be a similar situation the day after. It isn't just a numbers game though, in that the more good horses I ride out, the more chances I'll have of winning. If I turn down an opportunity to ride for trainers of this calibre, I experience feelings of guilt on a grand scale, not just for letting them down but for potentially letting myself down. Guilt can be a very damaging emotion for me and I try and avoid it at all costs.

My reward for saying yes, on the other hand, is that hopefully I'll get first refusal to ride the horses at a race if and when the time comes. What drives all of the above is an overwhelming desire to win, which is my lifeblood. My approach to this, however, is the proverbial double-edged sword as it's all-consuming. That's how I'm wired though. I can't help it. And what would the alternative be? Forcing myself not to care as much and to put in less effort? That's simply unthinkable.

I enjoyed watching the National last weekend, but not nearly as much as in years gone by. I know that the changes they've made have been done with the best of intentions, but it isn't the race it used to be. Watching the Grand National used to make my heart go at a hundred miles an hour and fill me full of adrenaline. Christmas morning had nothing on the National when I was growing up, and especially when my Uncle Jim was involved. In 2002, Jim won the Cheltenham Gold Cup and the Grand National, but it's his win in the latter, on the legendary Bindaree, that I remember most. The excitement was almost unbearable that day and resulted in a five-minute adrenaline rush that left me worried that I might explode. I was on a high for days after.

In those days, just to get a clear round at the National was an incredible achievement, but to win the race was out of this world. Thanks to the changes they've made, the National is now just a big field jumps handicap for high-quality horses. They certainly go very fast but the test of strength and stamina has been weakened thanks to the new jumps. For instance, I Am Maximus in this year's race jumped OK on the whole, but he made a few mistakes. Mistakes that in years gone by would have tested him and Paul Townend a lot more. Lesser the challenge, lesser the achievement. It's a great shame in my opinion, which I'm sure will be contentious. As I said though, I understand exactly why they capitulated. The Grand National is and always has been the anti-racing brigade's biggest weapon to use against the sport and so the temptation to blunt that weapon must have been too much.

While we're on the subject of National Hunt racing, it's always been an ambition of mine to win a jumps race, and on 5 December last year I was booked to ride an appropriately named Cian Collins-trained horse called Lets Do This in a three-and-a-half-mile novice handicap hurdle at Wincanton.

I remember being surprised by how much attention this received in the press and media at the time, but for a few days it was everywhere. I think I was probably a bit naive as I assumed that no one would really be that bothered. 'Your uncle's Jim Culloty and you're a three-time champion jockey,' a pal of mine said to me. 'What on earth did you expect?'

I've been harbouring the ambition to ride in a jumps race for a very long time and when I returned after my fourteen-month ban in February 2023 I decided to apply for a dual licence instead of just the Flat. The idea being, I think, that by having the licence in place I'd be more likely to do something about it. That almost happened a lot sooner than expected when I was tipped to ride in the Champion Bumper at the 2023 Cheltenham Festival, but that didn't work out in the end. Speaking of the Cheltenham Festival, when news about my ride at Wincanton was announced, one of the bookmakers – it was Coral, I think – reacted by making me 10/1 to ride a winner at this year's Cheltenham Festival. I wonder if anyone backed me?

Because of the way my brain works, from the moment I accepted the ride at Wincanton I started fretting about how it would all end and whether I'd end up just embarrassing myself. I got over that pretty quickly though. I'm an extraordinarily competitive individual and regardless of what made-up disasters my mind might be concocting, if horses are involved in a competitive environment my desire to finish first will always prevail – eventually! In this instance, as opposed to just winning, I also wanted to test myself and find out if I was good enough. Racing and hopefully winning over the jumps will be one of the final pieces of my own competitive equestrian jigsaw, the other being showjumping.

It's an ambition of mine that when I eventually retire as a jockey, I'll compete in some events. Not at the highest level (showjumping events are rated by stars (one to five) to indicate the level of difficulty and prize money). That would be too difficult, I think. I could probably aim for some three-star events though, such as the Nations Cup. I do take it seriously. In fact, before I decided to commit to becoming a professional jockey, I dreamed about becoming an international showjumper. I even went as far as learning to speak French and German, which would have allowed me to train with the very best people such as Marcus Ehning, who is my favourite rider. The idea of trying to do both at the highest standard did flash across my consciousness at one point, but only very briefly. Even if I'd had the talent, my intense approach to things wouldn't have allowed me to do both. It would have been the end of me.

If I do decide to give it a go after I retire, I'd have some pretty useful people around me. Richard Howley, who is number thirty-six in the world at the moment, is a very good friend of mine, as are the likes of Michael Duffy and Denis Lynch who are both in the top 100. Showjumping is taken very seriously across Europe and in the States, but now also in the Middle East. As the sport grows, so does my attraction to it so we'll have to see what happens. I have a mentor in Richard Howley, though, so if I do give it a go I'll stand the best possible chance of succeeding at some level.

In the end, the meeting at Wincanton was abandoned after heavy rain, so it all came to nothing. The ambition still burns and once this season is done and dusted I'll see where I am physically and mentally and then perhaps try again. I can't think about it until then though.

The catalyst for me making the decision to become a jockey and not a showjumper was, once again, down to my Uncle Jim. When I was eleven, my father decided to buy a farm in a place called Templemary which is in the parish of Buttevant in County Cork. The farm was adjacent to one of three farms that Jim had bought and had turned into an incredible training facility.

My ambition at the time with regards to horses was, as I've

already mentioned, to become an international showjumper. I watched a lot of racing on television (especially if Jim was on) but harboured no ambition at all to follow in his footsteps, either over the jumps or on the Flat.

About three years later, Jim asked me to ride out for him during the summer holidays. I'd be getting paid so I agreed. I already had a bit of an income from buying and selling ponies but this was something regular.

Although I thoroughly enjoyed riding out for Jim, the horses were too strong for me (I was still quite weak and small for my age) and the horses themselves were used to stronger and heavier riders. They were forever running off with me. As a consequence, and because I was keen to improve as a horseman, Jim arranged for me to start riding out for a local Flat trainer called Tommy Stack during the holidays. Mr Stack and his son Fozzy taught me how to ride a racehorse properly and I had a great time there. I was eventually able to repay some of their kindness in 2023 by riding a Group 1 winner for them at Belmont Park.

After leaving Tommy Stack's I went home to do my Leaving Certificates, which are the equivalent of A levels in Ireland, before going to ride out for Aidan O'Brien. I might not have been a racing fanatic necessarily (yet), but I was well aware of the stature of Aidan, not to mention many of his horses. I remember arriving at Ballydoyle for the first time and seeing both Camelot and St Nicholas Abbey almost immediately. I was like, *Wow, this is pretty cool!* My God, I was nervous though. Incredibly so.

I started off by riding some of Aidan's what you might call lesser horses, but in a short time I was riding work with the

likes of Joseph O'Brien, Seamie Heffernan and Colm Donoghue. At Ballydoyle, only riders who Aidan deems are good
enough are allowed to ride work on the gallops whereas the
rest do general exercise. Being put on the 'work list' by Aidan
himself meant that I was now good enough to be part of that
contingent and it was an incredibly proud moment. In fact,
looking back it was probably my first ever genuine professional achievement. The adrenaline rush it created was just
incredible. Similar to the one I experienced when Jim won
the National, just stronger as I was now directly involved.

What really struck me after being chosen by Aidan to ride
work was the effort he went to in order to help me improve
as a horseman. Almost every day he would critique my day's
performance as he inspected the horses in the evening and
would offer me advice in the most consultative and gracious
manner. 'You should have had your heels down a little bit
more today, Oisin,' he'd say. Or, 'Don't have such a tight rein
when you jump off.' Things like that. Considering how much
Aidan had going on, the fact that he managed to find time to
help the likes of me and had actually been observing me was
just extraordinary. He didn't need to do that and the enthusiasm it instilled in me as a consequence is something that
has never left me. I've been lucky enough to have worked
both for and with some hugely impressive people over the
years but to have had Aidan as an early mentor is something
very special indeed.

Something else I learned in Ireland during those early
days that left me in good stead for what was to come was the
importance of a healthy work ethic. While I was at Jim's I
used to muck out and then ride out prior to going to school.

I remember him putting the lights of his jeep on so I could exercise the horses while it was still dark. At Tommy Stack's I often used to have to walk to where I was living in Dualla after work as I didn't have my own transport and everyone would be off racing. It was only about four miles from Cashel but it used to test me sometimes when the weather was bad. Which it often was.

I've been trying to remember whether or not there was a eureka moment when I decided that I wanted to become a professional jockey and not a showjumper. In all honesty, I really can't remember, but I think it was more of an organic thing. The seed was probably planted when my Uncle Jim gave my family a horse in 2010 called Derby's Garden. During the following year I won on him no fewer than ten times which is when I must have caught the bug. As impressive as that sounds, it had far more to do with Derby's Garden than me. There were also quite a few other young riders coming through at the time who were better than I was. Riders such as Jack Kennedy who would go on to win the 2021 Cheltenham Gold Cup on Minella Indo. As opposed to being put off by this I allowed it to push me on and so when Jim asked me if I wanted to ride out for him during the holidays I said yes please. From there the enthusiasm just grew and by the time I got to Aidan's I was fairly sure that I wanted to do it professionally.

But as much as I have to credit Aidan for having mentored and enthused me in my early days as an aspiring jockey, and he did, the founder of the feast, so to speak, both in terms of sparking an initial interest in racing and then developing a work ethic, not to mention nurturing my skills as a horseman, was most definitely Jim. Having somebody of his stature and with his passion for racing as a member of your own family was impressive enough, even without him then helping to bring you on. When I finally realized that I did have a passion for racing, Jim encouraged me effusively and without him I would almost certainly be doing something else.

I'm often asked what I might have become had I not decided to work with horses. Well, my best subjects at school were German, Business and Economics, and French. The subject I was most interested in was Business and Economics and had I not taken an equestrian path in life I would probably have ended up becoming either an accountant or an entrepreneur of some kind. Accountancy is almost the family business on my mother's side as five of her seven siblings are qualified accountants.

Another question I'm occasionally asked is whether I have any regrets about not becoming a showjumper. Or should I say, not attempting to become a showjumper. The answer is, I don't. Partly because I enjoy what I do for a living at the moment immensely, despite what it takes out of me sometimes, and partly because I know how incredibly hard it is, not just to make it anywhere near the top as a showjumper, but then to stay there and then make a living out of it.

A good friend of mine is the showjumper Michael Duffy, whom I've already mentioned. He and I are a similar age and attended a lot of the same pony competitions when we were young. Through Michael I've seen first-hand what it takes to become a successful showjumper day to day and mark my words, it isn't for the faint-hearted. Not only do they have to ride very well but they have to buy and sell horses, run the business, manage staff and deal with all the injuries. It is a bit like being a trainer, I suppose, but you're your own first-choice jockey. The reason showjumping still operates this way is because it hasn't been a professional sport for very long and so the protagonists are still used to being self-contained.

The investment for things like equipment and infrastructure is also significant in showjumping. A horsebox alone can set you back half a million pounds plus, and a lot of the showjumpers I know have two. Then there are things such as arenas which obviously cost a fortune. Even the jumps themselves could easily set you back a hundred and fifty thousand pounds plus. The reason I mention this is because there is an assumption that showjumpers are all stinking rich, but that simply isn't the case.

It's different in racing. Horseboxes and the like don't cost anywhere near as much and it's the same with tack. The exercise tack for a racehorse might be worth a thousand pounds whereas the saddle alone for a showjumper could be worth five or six thousand. Also, a lot of trainers will have the use of facilities belonging to the Jockey Club that they can use for a nominal fee. In other words it's subsidized, unlike showjumping.

From my point of view, although I too completely rely on thoroughbred horses to be successful, unlike a showjumper all I have to do is get myself to the races on time, make sure I'm the correct weight, communicate effectively with the trainer and the owner, ride the horse, and then get back in the car and either drive or be driven away. I suppose another often applicable comparison would be parents and grandparents. Parents (showjumpers) have all the responsibility and worry and receive precious little thanks, whereas the grandparents (jockeys) just arrive on the scene every so often, stay for a wee while, have all the fun, take all the plaudits and then hand the grandkids back. It's like chalk and cheese when it comes to stress.

Anyway, I'd best crack on. I've an awful lot to do today and I've already gone on far too long.

THREE

Early Days

En route to Beverley Races

THE TWO DAYS AT NEWBURY I mentioned last time turned out to be a bit of a damp squib. Not once during any of the races did I feel like I could win. Subsequently, all of the adrenaline and excitement that's usually bubbling away somewhere never really materialized.

All of this is driven by you having options and then decisions to make during a race that will improve your chances of winning or at least being placed. Take them away and what do you have left? Nothing. After all, you're there to win.

It actually happens quite a lot as a jockey (horses running badly or not as expected) but usually in isolation. To have a run as bad as that though, eleven races in a row over two days, is almost unheard of for me. I don't mind admitting that it made me feel quite down for a day or two and it was only after I had ridden in a few races in which I felt I could challenge that normality was restored. Even then, regardless of the outcome, I'll often focus on my strike rate. It's still preferable to feeling uncompetitive.

On the upside, because I had very little stimulation either during or just after the meeting at Newbury, I slept very well. It's different when you're riding fancied horses that simply don't perform or on which you make a mistake. In fact, in terms of sleep, that has to be one of the worst situations of all. For me, at least. You have all the stimulation in the world after that yet it's driven mainly by anxiety. Believe me, it's not very soothing.

Epsom the following Tuesday was the antithesis of New-bury, both in terms of the results and my experiences, and in terms of my subsequent emotions. I rode a horse called Portsmouth in the last race that improved immeasurably having had his hood taken off. He was alert and responsive yet was able to relax so I had the best of both worlds. I also made sure that he didn't win by too far which will give him a chance of winning another few races. In the second race I won on a horse called Bellum Justum who is likely to have put himself in contention for the Derby. I loved riding him last year but could never understand why it took him so long to win. I got such a good feel from him though, especially in a race at Newmarket last September which he won.

Horses can put themselves in contention for winning an event such as the Derby by doing well in certain races known as trial races. A race called The Feilden Stakes at Newmarket is a popular trial race for the Derby, as is the Craven Stakes at the same course.

When cantering Bellum Justum, his stride isn't long so it feels like he's turning over quickly. Normally, this would signify that a horse is fast but can't stay, as a staying horse tends to have a longer action and a slower turnover. Anyway, because of the above I doubted that Bellum Justum would be able to perform over a mile and a quarter, which was the distance of today's race, and didn't hold out much hope. Fortunately I was wrong.

The pace of the race was slow at first and we only started racing at the seven-furlong start. I'm not sure what had changed but it was as though whatever had been holding him back had suddenly been removed and he shot off like a rocket. After crossing the line I tried to pull him up but he wouldn't stop, at least not at first. He wanted to keep going. I was delighted with him, as was Andrew Balding. I don't want to get too overexcited but he definitely could be a Derby candidate. Then again, if he doesn't stay a mile and a half I won't be too disappointed. I'll be looking forward to him coming back to a mile and a quarter and a mile again later on in the year.

Talking of the Classics, I should probably mention that in the 1,000 Guineas this year I'll be riding See The Fire for Andrew in favour of Porta Fortuna and the French filly, Ramatuelle. All three are obviously excellent horses but the thing that tipped me towards See The Fire is the sense of loyalty I feel towards Andrew, not to mention the owner, Jeff Smith. If it was simply down to which horse I thought stood the best chance of winning then Porta Fortuna would probably win the day, but only just. Andrew and Jeff have supported me through thick and thin and they more than deserve my loyalty.

See The Fire has been bred to do well from two to three and although she hasn't grown a lot, she had a good campaign as a two-year-old. If I'm being completely honest, I felt like I should have won the Fillies' Mile on her at Newmarket last year after having had what turned out to be a false reading from her on heavy ground over a mile at Doncaster the time before. In the Fillies' Mile I was looking for redemption and engaged her in a battle early on with Shuwari. Although Shuwari turned out to be the faster horse on the day, the battle we were having set the race up for Ylang Ylang who was off the bridle and just ran us down. As well as feeling loyalty to Jeff and Andrew, I feel like there's some unfinished business between me and See The Fire.

When it comes to the 2,000 Guineas I don't have a mount at the moment, but it's likely I'll ride a colt called Haatem for Richard Hannon. Haatem won the Craven which is often the best Guineas trial, but I still don't think he'll be good enough to win the big one. We'll see.

The thing that's been spending the most amount of time in my consciousness just recently is the fact that the start of the new champion jockey season is almost upon us. As I said earlier, the season runs from the Guineas Festival (Saturday 4 May) to what's called British Champions Day at Ascot on Saturday 19 October.

If I was given the choice, I'd rather win ten Group 1 races than the Jockeys Championship, but with the quality of horses I'm probably going to be riding, the former would seem like a bridge too far at the moment. Don't get me wrong, I'll be riding plenty of good horses, but some of the time a lot of my closest rivals will be riding better ones. That can all change, of course, and did last year, but I doubt it will to such an extent that it'll make a great deal of difference. Anyway, we'll see. You probably think I'm being overly negative but that's just the way my brain works. Despite me being an extremely competitive individual my competitiveness is often at odds with my glass being half empty. I'll tell you, nothing's ever straightforward with me.

On a positive note, I went to Wolverhampton this morning and rode out a beautiful unnamed two-year-old for Hugo Palmer who reminded me of a horse I had some success on for Andrew called South Seas. It's a few hours on now but I'm still buzzing from it, despite having ridden another three that were no good. I'm on my way to Beverley now for two rides and probably won't get home until half ten or quarter to eleven. Then I'll be up tomorrow morning at 5.30am to ride out for David Menuisier in East Sussex before heading off to Sandown where I've got 8st 8lb. I'm probably 8st 12lb at the moment and won't have much time to sweat so it'll be touch and go. I'm not worried though.

I probably won't eat now before this evening and all I've had today so far is 300ml of water and no coffee. I'll probably drink another 200ml before I get to Beverley. I know it must sound bonkers us having to measure out what we drink, but water is weight at the end of the day. Half a litre of water weighs more than a pound so every drop counts.

I have my running gear with me and will run and walk two laps of the track when I get there, depending on my energy levels, which will be three miles in all. I'll probably feel quite flat after the two rides. Unless I have a winner, of course, which I doubt I will unfortunately. Either way, I should sleep OK as I'll be pretty exhausted. My meal this evening, by the way, will consist of some oranges and a few grapes.

I have an update on the Italian fine situation. Having spoken to a few people it seems like I might have to just bite the bullet and cough up, which is incredibly infuriating and feels like an insult. The original fine four years ago was

€1,000 but with the lawyer fees and everything else it's come out at €5,000. Although I feel quite bitter about it I also feel sad because at one point some of the best racehorses in the world were in Italy and the racing itself was something that the country could be proud of. And look at some of the horsemen they've produced. Frankie Dettori, Marco Botti and Andrea Atzeni, to name a few. There's also a very good Italian trainer in France at the moment called Mario Baratti whom I won a Group 3 for last year. Some of the racecourses too are just beautiful. They have a rich history and a huge amount of talent but the industry itself has gone to pot somewhat. I'm not sure why, exactly. Bad management and a lack of funding, most probably. And this is not sour grapes, by the way. My conviction and fine, although unsafe and unfair, are nothing more than an inconvenience really, whereas what's happened to the Italian horse racing industry as a whole is nothing less than a tragedy.

FRIDAY, 3 MAY 2024

En route from Kingsclere to Lambourn

I've been riding out for Andrew this morning and it occurred to me just now as I got in the car to come home that I haven't told you the story of how we started working together.

As far as I know, the initial discussion about me moving to England was between my parents and my Uncle Jim. While I thought I'd done quite well for Aidan, his children were riding for him at the time and with him not having many low-grade horses it would have been tough to get going. We all aspire to ride quality but in order to get to that position you need quantity first. 'There would be far more opportunities for Oisin over in England,' he said to my Uncle Jim.

One of the reasons Andrew's name was suggested as an alternative was because he'd already had both William Buick and David Probert as apprentices in recent years and they were doing really well. Uncle Jim was also quite friendly with Andrew so it kind of made sense. The only potential pitfall, as far as I know, at least initially, was that Andrew already had quite a few apprentices at the time, but he was eventually persuaded to say yes.

When it was first suggested to me that I might move over to England, I froze. The prospect of working for Andrew and becoming an apprentice jockey to such a successful trainer was a dream come true, but I'd only been abroad twice before in my entire life – once to England for a wedding and once to Spain for a holiday – and I was incredibly nervous about it. So much so that had I been a little bit braver, I might have said something and asked to stay put. As it was, I think I knew deep down that despite the trepidation I was feeling it was something I needed to do, not just for my professional development but my personal development too. I was a wee bit wet behind the ears.

Such is the appalling state of my memory (not to mention the fact that I've done a fair bit of travelling since) I actually can't remember whether I got the ferry or a plane over to England. Regardless of which, I arrived at Kingsclere for the first time in mid-October 2012. The weather was just dreadful I remember and as undulating and picturesque as the surrounding countryside is at Kingsclere, it made me feel even worse.

The number of apprentice jockeys that Andrew had under him at the time hadn't been made clear to me before travelling and when I found out it was ten I felt a bit sick. All of them had arrived before me and most of them were older than me. I was already quite competitive but the prospect of being the youngest and least experienced apprentice in such a big group felt very daunting. *How on earth am I going to get rides?* I thought to myself.

For the first couple of months I was ridiculously homesick and would ring my mother and Uncle Jim at every opportunity telling them that I wanted to come home. I remember Jim saying to me that this was my big opportunity and that I needed to stick at it. 'The homesickness will wear off soon enough,' he assured me. Of course, as well as having been through something similar himself, Jim would have known literally hundreds of people who had been through it too. He knew what he was talking about.

That first Christmas was by far the most difficult time. I'd never spent one without my family before and I remember feeling very sad. Luckily, there were a few people at Kingsclere in exactly the same boat as me which made a difference.

I forget how long it took me to start feeling better but it was hastened by the fact that Anna Lisa Balding is one of the most maternal human beings I've ever met and her ability to make homesick and nervous young men and women feel safe, welcome and cared for is extraordinary. I didn't say very much to her at the start. I didn't say much to anybody! I didn't need to though. It was more about what she said to me. Words of reassurance and encouragement generally, which was exactly what I needed.

My improvement in mood was also hastened by the friends I made at Kingsclere, not least Kieren Shoemark and Rob Hornby who arrived a short time before me and who lived either side of me in the hostel. Tom Brown, who went on to win the John Smith's Cup at York in 2016 and later became a paramedic after suffering an injury, also became a good friend of mine. He was an absolute legend – a big brother really – and used to drive us around the place.

Leisure time was often spent on the Equicizer (a mechanical horse used for building strength, skill and balance) while watching the racing and chatting, or in the evenings we'd go running in the indoor school. Kieren was a much better runner than Rob and me and he got us fit by trying to keep up with him. We also used to fight quite a lot, as young lads do. I remember one day Kieren and I tried to play a game of tennis together (we were both worse than useless) and unfortunately it ended up in fisticuffs. I remember Kieren pinning me to the ground. 'Stop struggling and I'll let you go,' he said to me, which I agreed to. I then attacked him, as you would, and pinned him to the ground. The tennis court at Kingsclere is situated in between the stables and the main house which overlooks it and if Andrew or Anna Lisa had seen us we'd have been for it.

Anna Lisa was in charge of the discipline among the apprentices at Kingsclere and made sure that we were always well turned out and that we tidied our rooms. And there was no insubordination or answering back. While Anna Lisa can be a very maternal person, you also wouldn't want to get on the wrong side of her. As well as wanting order at the stables though, she was trying to give us a grounding for later life. We all appreciated the fact.

My relationship with Andrew was almost non-existent at the start, save for a couple of words when coming off the gallops or when he was around the stables. At the end of the day it was his job to break me in as a jockey, not as a young man who was away from home for the first time and settling into new surroundings.

One of the first actual conversations I had with Andrew was when he informed me in March 2013 that he was sending me away to apply for my licence. This is what I'd been work-ing towards for the best part of three years and although I felt euphoric, I was relieved more than anything. There were friends of mine over in Ireland such as Connor King who'd been riding winners since they were sixteen and a lot of my fellow apprentices at Andrew's who had recently got their licences were starting to do the same. Dan Muscutt, Tom Brown, Joey Haynes. They were all going great guns and I desperately wanted to follow suit. But in addition to this, there was normally a big waiting list for the jockey licence course and only a couple of intakes a year which had also been playing on my mind.

The course is residential and lasts a week, and one of the first things they covered when I arrived was race riding. This, as I remember it, involved watching lots of replays of races involving careless riding incidents. After that we did some basic maths and English lessons which fortunately I'd already covered at school and found easy. I appreciate not everybody attending the licence course will have had a full formal edu-cation, but everyone on my intake had as far as I could tell and it seemed like a waste of time. It was so rudimentary.

What was a lot harder were the fitness tests. We started off with what are known as bleep tests which are designed to measure your aerobic capacity. They're very basic and involve running back and forth between two lines while keeping pace with a series of beeps. The time between beeps decreases over time requiring the participant to increase their speed.

I'd say that roughly half the people who were on my intake failed at this juncture. You might think that's a bit strange as jockeys have to be fit, but being fit to ride is a lot different to being fit to run. This is something I didn't quite understand at the time. The people who were sent home were obviously fit enough to ride a horse (had they not been they wouldn't have been there in the first place), yet because they couldn't run for that long they were failed. It felt strange to me. Anyway, the rest of the course mostly involved working on the Equicizer and on real horses and I went back to Kingsclere obviously hoping that I'd done enough.

I think it took about a week before the BHA confirmed that I'd passed the course and once again the pervading emotion I felt on finding out was relief. Incidentally, the only other apprentice from my intake who I know for sure passed the course was Hector Crouch. He's had an excellent 2024 so far and is odds-on to win his first Group 1. I hope he does.

The change from being an apprentice to being a working apprentice is vast. One minute you haven't a care in the world really (apart from how long it'll take you to become a working jockey, which is ironic) and the next you're worrying about your weight and how you're going to get to and from race meetings. As an apprentice jockey my day consisted of riding out four or five lots in the morning, watching racing on TV and then doing evening stables (feeding, mucking out and grooming the horses). That was basically it. I was busy enough, but it was all a bit one-dimensional and repetitious. Then, once I started as a working jockey, boom! My feet didn't touch the ground.

At the start of my career I couldn't drive so was always relying on lifts. That was probably my biggest stress in the early days. Well, that and the weight. The journey time to a meeting would determine how many lots I could ride out before setting off but it wasn't an exact science and sometimes I'd get it wrong. I was never actually late for a race but I had a few close calls. It's a horrible feeling having to rely on other people to get to do your job. You're obviously not in control and if it all goes belly up you'll often have no alternative. As somebody who is used to and enjoys being in charge of their own destiny, this used to bother me big time.

Part of me used to believe, just occasionally, that it might be easier if I had just a ride or two a week. In hindsight, though, the baptism of fire that I experienced in those early days put me in good stead and if I had my time again I wouldn't change a thing. Being a busy jockey was everything I'd dreamed of and because I was getting so many rides I knew the winners would come. And they did. Had I been riding two a week, that progress wouldn't have been there and that would have upset me a lot more.

One thing I was very conscious of in my early days was the need to not only maintain my work rate, but appreciate the importance of not taking things for granted. I'd heard lots of stories about young jockeys having success at the start of their careers but then it tapering off, probably because they got too comfortable. Once success feels like habit it's easy for that to happen. It takes place subliminally, I think, the same as becoming addicted to cigarettes or alcohol. You don't really think about it when you start and then all of a sudden you're addicted. This is the reverse effect in that it results in less as opposed to more, but it's the same principle.

Maintaining some self-awareness is incredibly important in your early days and if you snooze, the chances are you'll lose.

A big help for me back in those days was that I was still working at Kingsclere so when I wasn't racing I still had responsibilities at the yard. This was just the leveller I needed really, not only professionally but also personally. It was my home at the time and the majority of my friends were there.

A good illustration of how this contrast benefitted me would be the Gold Cup meeting at Ayr in September 2013. As well as winning the main race on Highland Colori, I rode three additional winners, and despite them all having accumulated odds of 9,260/1. The following day I was all over the back of the papers but had a full day's work to do at the stables and just got on with it. I'm obviously not suggesting that I'd have gone off the rails if I hadn't had to do that, but it allowed me to appreciate the enormity of what had happened in a safe and quiet environment. I had a ride at Leicester on the Monday and went on to have another winner.

Anyway, that's my early days at Kingsclere covered.

On Tuesday I had a very good win for Andrew on a horse called Run Away in a fillies' maiden at Yarmouth. I first rode her just over a year ago in Ireland. I was over there riding breeze-up horses and got a call from Mick Murphy at Longways Stables. 'We've got this filly,' he said. 'She's a full sister to Blackbeard who won the Prix Morny and the Middle Park at Newmarket. She was sold last year for €2.6million at the Goffs Orby Sale but the buyer didn't cough up so she's back on the market. Come and have a look at her, will you. I'd like your opinion.'

When I arrived at Longways Stables, Mick confessed that he hadn't been able to do much with her so far but she was definitely strong and bright. She had a bit of a cough when I was there so I wasn't able to press too many buttons. Mick was right though, she was as strong as an ox and very powerful.

After chatting again to Mick, I got on the phone to Sheikh Fahad and recommended that he try and buy her. In turn, he got on the phone to the insurance magnate David Howden and Henri Bozo who owns Monceaux Stud in France and they managed to do a deal. I'm not sure how much she cost in the end but she wouldn't have been cheap. It was also a slow process getting her this far as a lot of people had been asking where she'd been and why she hadn't run yet. Also, some of her work when I hadn't ridden her had been very ordinary apparently and people had worried that she might be no good. Whenever I'd ridden her she'd always given me a fantastic feel and her work last Saturday, so a few days before the race, had been incredible. I mean, really top class. She felt superb.

On the day of the race she drifted from 7/4 favourite to 9/1, which was a bit strange. David Howden sent me a WhatsApp asking me what was going on. 'Is everything OK?' he said. 'As far as I know,' I replied. 'Don't let it worry you. I think she'll win.'

The race itself started inauspiciously as she almost fell out of the stalls. To be fair she'd been in there for some time waiting for the others, but it still came as a surprise. I'd never put her through the stalls myself but she'd been through a few nights before and had flown out. The fact that she'd dropped so far in the betting had been playing on my mind and without wanting to appear paranoid, the only feasible explanation I could think of was that not enough people had faith in her. On some days that might have affected me adversely but not today. I'd probably ridden Run Away at least twenty times over the past year and had complete confidence in her, even if the punters didn't. Anyway, after the somewhat dodgy start we caught the leaders quickly, led from two furlongs out and won by a good neck. She'll go on to good things, that horse.

I must say I'm looking forward to the weekend. See The Fire hasn't enjoyed a perfect preparation though. She was a bit behind in her coat until recently (at this time of year horses go from having their winter coat to their summer coat and horses that have their summer coat tend to be in better physical shape) and back in March had been a bit under the weather. In the past four weeks, however, everything's been fine and I can only hope that she's ready. Her last two pieces of work would certainly indicate that she's there or thereabouts. The thing is, although you press plenty of buttons during these sessions, you're not getting everything out of a horse. You can only do that at the races. She's fifth in the betting at the moment and deserves to be a place or two higher in my opinion. We've been drawn near Fallen Angel whom I know well and wanted to be close to, so that's good.

So, how have I been in myself just lately? I was in bad form yesterday evening. I got a lot of plaudits for winning on Coltrane at Ascot for Andrew, but felt I should have won afterwards on a horse called Docklands for Harry Eustace. It was a Listed mile race and in hindsight I should have given him a wake-up call rather than going easy on him late on. I was still pushing and giving him taps but what I should have done is grab hold of him. Unfortunately, that was the difference between winning and losing and I felt absolutely dreadful afterwards. In fact, it was only after having counselling yesterday that I was able to process it all properly and start to move on. The only thing more soul-destroying than losing a race because a horse hasn't performed well is when you, the jockey, make a mistake. It's the worst feeling of all.

It's probably fair to say that I'm my own worst critic and can be very hard on myself sometimes. That said, I always make sure I come away from a situation like this having learned something, which is the main thing. I don't give a damn what the so-called experts say as more often than not I don't think they're right. They usually either have an agenda of some sort or aren't in full possession of the facts which obviously clouds their judgement. Either way, it all goes over my head.

FRIDAY, 10 MAY 2024

Lambourn

I'm going through a bit of a nightmare at the moment. I've had no fewer than seven second places since my last winner and it's starting to play on my mind. Some of the horses have run above expectation, some have run below, and some have been a bit unlucky. I just keep on hitting the crossbar.

It's affecting my sleep a bit, which is to be expected, but what I cannot allow to happen is for it to affect my confidence. If I do, I might start changing the way I ride which would be a disaster. I know people who've done that during a lean spell before and it never ends well. It's an easy trap to fall into, though. After wracking your brains day after day, you come to the conclusion that a root and branch change is necessary and in the process you alter the way you ride, forget who you really are and come out a lot worse. I just have to keep my head down and try and treat every day and every race like a brand new opportunity.

Speaking of which.

I'm at Chester this evening for four rides and have a chance in every race. Aztec Empire is favourite in the Chester Cup, but I'm doubtful about him as he's been off a while. The ground also probably won't be ideal for him unfortunately. They haven't had any rain up in Chester for a while and didn't water the track last night so it'll be very fast. Too fast, perhaps.

Prior to my fourteen-month suspension, in situations like these when I was on a bad run of form, I'd have reached for the alcohol. I was about to say that the alcohol would enable me to deal with what was happening, whereas in truth it simply allowed me to forget about it. That was what I wanted, though. To forget.

After persuading myself that I couldn't deal with not riding winners all the time, which is what used to happen, I'd start to drink. The more I drank the less it mattered and eventually I would pass out. That would happen most nights during the height of my drinking and as opposed to just reaching for the alcohol during a run of bad form, I would reach for it every time I rode a horse that didn't win, which was virtually every day. Even on the very few occasions when I did have a day of winners, I'd celebrate by having a drink or ten.

Learning how to deal with issues such as this, which are part and parcel of being a jockey, without resorting to alcohol has been incredibly hard. Partly because I like alcohol I suppose, but also because I had never had to cope with things like this without the help of alcohol and so there was nothing (or nowhere) to attempt to get back to. That was my normality. The only attraction was the escapism alcohol brought and what it did for me. Does that make sense?

As difficult as it can be dealing with lean times such as these, the alternative of giving in to alcohol, although tempting on occasion, and especially when I'm going through a particularly bad run of form, is unthinkable. That's quite a bold statement coming from a not-long recovering alcoholic, but it's the truth. If the process of me drinking in order to avoid having to deal with difficult situations returns, that'll be the end of my career. It would also be deserved and all of my own doing. There's no question about that and my mindset each morning is to get through that day with no drink.

As is so often the case with addicts, being found out or being exposed as an addict is very often the best thing that can happen as it gives you the opportunity to seek help which will hopefully become a stepping stone to, or a platform for recovery. The only thing that worries me slightly is that if this losing streak carries on much longer, I'll be in uncharted territory and so the temptation to drink will become stronger. That's just me catastrophizing though, which is yet another consequence of how my brain is wired. The most likely outcome is that I'll get a winner or two over the weekend, but let's see.

In terms of British racing, one of the saddest things to happen this week was the Godolphin horse, Hidden Law, breaking down shortly after winning the Cheshire Vase on Wednesday and suffering a fatal injury. He was a very athletic and nimble sort of horse and when he took off at the bottom of the straight he was flying. According to his trainer, Charlie Appleby, he put in a false step when crossing the road after the line and landed badly. He sustained a fracture to his right front foreleg and had to be put to sleep. I was behind him at the time and until the crossing he looked fine. Then, two strides later he broke down. I feel terrible for the horse, of course, but also for William Buick, Charlie and the groom who looked after him. It's just one of those terrible accidents that you cannot legislate for unfortunately.

Because of my experiences with all things equine, and because I'm a realist, horses dying unexpectedly is an uncomfortable subject that I'm comfortable discussing. I've witnessed horses breaking down in their own stable before when they get cast and I've also witnessed them breaking down when they're out in the field having a pick of grass. All of a sudden they have a canter and a play and that's it. I saw the break with Hidden Law and I knew immediately that there was no recovery from that. William was very distraught. When you're doing the right thing, which he had been, and something like that happens, it's gut-wrenching. The fact that it happened to a very high-class horse makes it worse as he was a horse that racing fans could have followed and he had a bright career in front of him.

Anyway, let's move on.

What else have I been doing this week? I was in France on Monday but just for the one race. He was well beaten but has potential. He was waiting a bit for the other horses (colts often have an issue with concentration) so we'll try blinkers on him next time. Hopefully that will help to eke out some improvement.

Another thing that's been playing on my mind a bit this week, although less so as time has gone on, is the disappointment of Guineas weekend. See The Fire didn't run well at all and finished twelfth. The tempo of the race was quite strong which might have caught her out, but I thought she'd be bang in the mix. What's slightly frustrating is that I could have ridden the second, third and fourth in that race. Thank God none of them won, otherwise the frustration would be tenfold. In that respect, you have to feel sorry for James Doyle who was unable to ride the eventual winner, Elmalka, as he was riding over in France. At the same time I was very happy for his replacement, Silvestre De Sousa. Silvestre was coming back from a long suspension and he did a fine job. In fact, it's his first ever Classic winner, which makes the whole thing a bit of a fairy tale.

The same thing happened to me, of course, as just three months after returning from my own suspension last year I won the 1,000 Guineas on Mawj for Godolphin. I'd actually almost forgotten about that which sounds incredibly blasé. It's the nature of the beast, however, because as long as you remain active as a jockey you're only ever as good as your last win and at the moment I'm finding them increasingly difficult to come by.

Although I didn't have a ride in it, I thought the 2,000 Guineas was a very strong race indeed. The first and second, Notable Speech and Rosallion, are two horses that racing fans can follow through the year and get excited about as they are two supreme and out of the ordinary horses.

THURSDAY, 16 MAY 2024

York

My drought of winners finally and thankfully came to an end at Chester shortly after my last entry which obviously

came as a huge relief. The first horse, Mina Rashid, benefitted from a very strong pace and the second, City Streak,
was helped inadvertently by a non-runner. The non-runner
was one of Roger Varian's and was withdrawn because of the
ground. In fact, it ended up being a much easier race than
it ought to have been. Then, at Ascot on Saturday, I won
a fillies' handicap on a horse called Warda Jamila who is a
half-sister to Coltrane. She won't stay extreme distances and
it was important that she won.

On Sunday I spent eleven hours in the car, but it was worth
it as I came away from Newcastle with four wins. That's happened to me twice before up there but I had six in a day at
Tokyo once. It's not uncommon that if I ride a winner early
on in the card I'll ride at least another one.

At Windsor on Monday I had four rides and was conscious not to allow myself to get too carried away with what
had taken place on Friday and over the weekend. Whereas
it's easy for me to get bogged down by not having winners,
the reverse can also be true sometimes. Not because I ever
feel invincible or anything; I most certainly don't. You're
only ever as good as the horses you have underneath you,
give or take, so if I did adopt an air of invincibility I'd soon
be brought down to earth again. What I actually mean is
that it's easy to get carried away by the feelings and emotions
that winning can induce and you can start taking everything
a little bit lightly if you're not careful.

One of the races at Windsor on Monday ended up making
the headlines. I was about to ride a horse for Hugo Palmer
called He's Got Game in a Class 5 mile handicap when he
collapsed out of the stalls. I was flung forward in the saddle
and as his nose slid along the grass I started saying a Hail

Mary to myself. His legs just buckled for some reason but he may have taken a bad step. I've seen the exact same kind of incident occur with two jockeys before (Graham Lee and Tye Angland) and it's almost as terrifying to watch as it is to be part of. Not quite though.

I ended up getting a lot of praise for that race and it's had hundreds of thousands of views on social media. The fact is though that the horse stood up of his own accord, thank God. What's probably more impressive from my point of view is what happened afterwards as we actually went on to win the race. Normally after giving up so much ground you wouldn't stand a chance of getting placed in a race like that, let alone winning. He's Got Game wasn't done though. I could feel that from the moment he was up and it was almost as if he was annoyed with himself and wanted to make amends. Crucially, I managed not to lose either iron and with a furlong or so to go we were in with a chance. Then, with just under half a furlong left we got carried left by the eventual runner-up. Fortunately, I managed to push him forward one final time and we won by a head.

I arrived in York on Wednesday for the first day of the Dante meeting and got off to a great start by winning on a gorgeous bay filly called Secret Satire for Andrew in the Tattersalls Musidora Stakes which is a Group 3. I'm not saying it was an easy race but she's not a difficult filly to settle once she gets cover and she relaxed into a good rhythm very quickly. John Gosden's filly Friendly Soul underperforming didn't do our chances any harm. She was the 8/11 favourite but was nowhere to be seen. What I was especially happy with was Secret Satire's demeanour in the final furlong. It felt like she wasn't trying her hardest. She was just flicking her ear and waiting for the other horses. There's plenty more to come from her, that's for sure. Then again, for her to be a live Oaks contender she'll have to improve a lot and I'll tell you why.

The runner-up, a Charlie Johnston horse called Francophone, raced at Southwell a couple of Sundays ago and I almost beat her on a filly called Battle Queen for Andrew. In fact, we really should have won that race but she pulled up in front. My point being that Battle Queen is rated 80 so if she can give the likes of Francophone a run for her money, Secret Satire hasn't yet had to deal with Classic-winning material.

It's like a holiday being up at these meetings as there's no riding out to be done and far fewer distractions. In fact, this morning I didn't even wake up until gone 8am which would almost be unheard of back at home in Lambourn. You still have the pressure of making the weights and riding the horses, of course, but a nice lie-in and a minimal amount of travel and distraction is always very welcome. I adore York. It's steeped in history and is so picturesque. I've rented a beautiful town house about two miles from the track for the duration of the meeting as I have my mother with me as well as my Great Uncle Frank.

I've been reading in the papers recently about the tragic death of the retired jumps jockey Michael Byrne, who apparently committed suicide aged just thirty-six. I never met Michael but when somebody from the racing world takes their own life, it always leaves an indelible mark on the sport. Thirty-six years old, though. That is so, so sad.

What's especially tragic about Michael's death, but also slightly alarming, is that two of his closest friends, fellow retired jumps jockeys Liam Treadwell and James Banks, also took their own lives back in 2020. That's three retired jockeys in their thirties and with their lives in front of them. It can't just be a coincidence, surely. We go from chasing a dream to nothing, basically overnight, and it's very difficult to fill that void. I had a glimpse of it during my suspension and what stopped me getting sucked in was that I had something to look forward to and work towards. Nicky Henderson's daughter, Camilla, who is a renowned sports psychologist, has spoken about this on social media and hopefully it will start a conversation. It's one that needs to be had, I think.

We're two weeks into the Flat Jockeys Championship season and I'm where I want to be which is top of the table. As always, when you're in that position, there's only one way you can go and that's down, but I'm going to do everything in my power to remain there, you can be sure about that.

What's on my mind slightly more at the moment is the prospect of trying to achieve the difficult balance of remaining competitive in the championship while at the same time giving myself the best chance to win as many Group races as possible.

For those who aren't sure what Group races are or how they came about, let me quickly fill you in. About fifty years ago, the main horse racing nations in Europe put together a framework specifying where and when each of the country's most elite races should be staged, the idea being to avoid schedule clashes and the like. That framework became known as 'The Pattern' and the hierarchy of races that sit within that are Group 1, Group 2 and Group 3.

Group 1 races obviously represent the best of the best and are run off level weights, save for an allowance for mares and fillies against colts and geldings and three-year-old horses

over older horses. Group 2 races are still significant inter-
nationally, whereas Group 3 races are mainly of domestic
importance.

Finding the right balance between giving yourself the
best chance of winning both the championship and as many
Group races as possible is not an exact science – far from
it – and temptations arise from both sides. That said, unless
you're doing very well in the championship the temptation
to ride in a big race abroad, for instance, will always be a lot
stronger than the temptation to go and ride six at Newcastle
on a wet Tuesday evening. After all, in twenty years' time
when I'm no longer a jockey and am sitting on the couch
watching Chelsea play Arsenal, the races I'll want to look
back on will be the former and not the latter.

The final consideration is trying to manage other people's expectations and maintain the status quo. For instance,
Andrew has a lot of good runners coming up at Salisbury
today and then at Newmarket tomorrow and on Saturday,
but because I'm at York today and tomorrow and then at
Newbury on Saturday I'm unable to ride any of them. Financially it doesn't make any difference as the prize-money
percentages aren't that great for jockeys, but I'll probably
miss out on some winners, not to mention riding horses that
I know well and have helped get to this point. I'll give you
yet another example of how the race calendar can split your
loyalties as a jockey.

Chaldean's half-sister, Kassaya, is running at Salisbury
today and I'd much rather be riding her than the horses I've
got at York, none of which stand a chance in my opinion,
and it's the same on Saturday and Sunday. On Saturday a
horse called Hopeful is running at Newmarket. It's only a

handicap but she's a gorgeous filly. Well bred and stands a chance.

Although I won't be riding them I obviously hope that these horses of Andrew's win; not only because I want his stable form to remain on a high but because if these horses do well I will hopefully get to ride them some time in the future and in better races.

With regards to York and Newbury, my hand has been forced slightly as if I didn't agree to partner these horses I'd be letting some very influential people down. People with whom I have a good working relationship and have been successful. You see what I mean? It's a constantly moving dilemma.

THURSDAY, 23 MAY 2024

Lambourn

As I mentioned last time, I've had my mother and my Great Uncle Frank over to stay with me this past week or so. Great Uncle Frank is in his mid-seventies, has never married, has no children and is very Irish. He's also very abrupt, very direct and has a wicked sense of humour. He's kept me entertained, that's for sure. It's been great having them around.

So much for the prediction that my rides at York and Newbury wouldn't come to very much. Literally a few hours after recording my last entry I won the Yorkshire Cup on Giavellotto for Marco Botti. Then, at Newbury on the Sunday I won a Group 3 on Middle Earth for John and Thady Gosden which is by Roaring Lion out of Roheryn. Wins are always welcome but unexpected Group wins are especially sweet.

The favourite for the Yorkshire Cup was Aidan O'Brien's Tower Of London that beat Giavellotto last time out in Saudi. In that race, Tower Of London had been nine pounds better off whereas this time we only had to concede three pounds. I still wasn't sure if that was going to be enough, though. Giavellotto can often get a bit frazzled at the start of a race and then immediately start pulling. He didn't though, not this time. Also, Tower Of London didn't fire for some reason, which obviously did our cause no harm at all.

One thing I learned about Giavellotto from that race is that he's not that strong a stayer. He has a lot of pace though, which can often develop over time with those bigger horses. Coltrane was one. I remember riding him as a three-year-old. He didn't have many gears back then but as he got older he got stronger and then faster.

The Yorkshire Cup is a race that means quite a bit to me. Not only is it good prize money but together with the Dante it's the feature race of the meeting. Winning that and then the Group 3 at Newbury demonstrates the turnaround in fortunes that you can experience as a jockey. One minute I'm bemoaning the fact that I'm potentially missing out on a couple of winners in ordinary races at Salisbury and Newmarket and the next I'm unexpectedly winning Group races at York and Newbury. It's a metaphor for the sport itself. You never know what's around the corner.

Middle Earth was extremely fresh in the paddock, which was hardly surprising really as it was his first run in over two hundred days. He didn't scare exactly but he was definitely showing his exuberance. When he came out of the stalls I thought the race was over. He stood to break well but when I asked him to move he was as slow as hell which left us right at the back of the field and on the inside, which wasn't ideal. I just had to sit there and suffer. From two furlongs out we finally began to make headway and a furlong later we were second and just two lengths down. I wasn't sure if he'd manage to keep on but he did and we won by a nose. I was very impressed and am excited about how he might get on at Royal Ascot. I think he stands a chance in the Hardwicke.

Today was supposed to be a rare day off for me but so far it's been anything but. I'm down to go to Haydock at the weekend but the weather is going to be atrocious which has thrown up all kinds of questions. Which horses might be declared, which horses might handle the ground. It's one of those inevitable situations that's difficult to plan for and could become a nightmare. If Haydock ends up being abandoned I'll probably switch to York or Salisbury and it's up to my agent to keep in touch with the trainers and ensure that if that happens I'll be set up with some rides. It's pretty stressful for everyone concerned. I live and work in England though, mainly, and in England it rains from time to time.

The role of a jockey's agent is multi-faceted and they're just as important to our day-to-day existence as valets. In addition to booking rides for a jockey, an agent will help to select horses, arrange transport, book accommodation, sort out your expenses and schedule things such as interviews and appearances. They also deal with a lot of your business affairs and keep records of the race meetings you attend and make sure you meet all the regulatory requirements. Their knowledge of the sport, particularly form, is matched only by their knowledge of the jockeys they represent.

My agent, Gavin Horne, started working with me in 2015 and has been behind every Group 1 success I've ever had in the UK and Europe (I use a different agent in Japan and America) as well as one or two of the international ones. It's hard to put into words just how important an agent is to a jockey. As with a valet, they give us peace of mind and allow us to concentrate on the job in hand. Without them, life would be chaos.

Gavin looks after just me, Cieren Fallon and Nicola Currie and he is completely dedicated to our professional and personal development. He used to look after Shane Kelly so I was extremely lucky when he agreed to take me on. That was over ten years ago now and we've never had so much as a cross word. Sometimes one of us will choose the wrong horse but that's just a part of life. We'd never hold it against each other. Gavin lives over in Cambodia but even with the time difference we make the relationship work.

Trying to get good rides for a young jockey who has only just finished their apprenticeship and has no Group wins to their name must have been a thankless task at times, especially when you consider the amount of competition there was when I turned pro. I shudder to think how many phone calls Gavin must have made on my behalf over the years. Tens of thousands probably. He stuck with it though and together we've won three championships so far as well as a hundred-odd Group races. He's like a brother to me.

I do find the unpredictability of the sport hard to deal with sometimes. It's in my nature to want to give myself the best possible chance of winning on every occasion and the more variables there are (especially variables that you cannot control such as the weather) the more likely I am to lose. Yet again, that's part and parcel of the sport but that doesn't stop it affecting me.

I'm often advised to try and relax a bit more and take things one day at a time. Live in the moment and all that. It's certainly good advice but the only thing that's going to get me out of bed in the morning after four hours' sleep and having spent ten or twelve hours in the car the day before is the prospect of working a couple of well-bred two-year-olds that have a bright future ahead of them. A bright future with me.

I'll give you another example.

There's a chance I'll be riding at Saratoga Race Course in New York on 7 and 8 June. Those horses will all be carrying light weights so I'm already questioning whether or not I'll be able to do the weight and whether or not it'll be worth it. In other words, the hamster wheel never stops turning. I have no idea what a normal athlete or sportsperson does on their day off, but so far this morning, in addition to pondering all of the above, I've been looking at weather reports, checking the international entries and watching race replays, and it's only 10am. Another piece of advice I'm often given is to try and delegate more, but that's almost impossible. What I do begins and ends with me, from wasting to riding the horses. Everything I can delegate I do.

An actual day off, as in sitting around doing nothing, would be quite dangerous for me as it would probably result in me mulling over all the things that were bothering me at that point in time. Instead of coming out of it feeling refreshed I'd feel frazzled so it's best to keep on moving, at least a little bit. It's just too big a contrast. Sure, we have to take care of ourselves, but you also have to take care of your business. Yet again it's all about seeking the right balance.

I was asked the other day whether or not there is anyone in either my social or professional circle whom I can offload to about all of this. I've already stated that you would never let on to a fellow jockey about your worries or mental frailties and it's the same with a trainer. In order for a trainer to want to employ you they have to have faith in you and so showing signs of weakness would put you at a serious disadvantage. The only exception I can think of when you might confide in a fellow jockey is when you're going through something specific that the other can definitely relate to, such as a careless riding suspension.

'What do you think? Should I appeal?'

From a purely racing point of view, the closest thing I have to a confidant would be my agent, Gavin. He sees everything unfold in real time from entries to the weather and probably knows more about my day-to-day professional life than anyone else on earth. For anything that's not racing-related I have my manager, Jimmy Derham. Jimmy's a sound fella, is intelligent and looks after my financial affairs and the like. I have complete faith in both Jimmy and Gavin and am lucky to have them looking out for me.

Regardless of what happens on Saturday at Haydock, on Sunday I'll be going over to Ireland. There's a fillies' maiden happening there that a friend of mine called Peter Trainor sponsors. He also has a half-share in one of the runners and I want to show my support.

FOUR

The Weighing Room

Lambourn

MANAGING YOUR EXPECTATIONS EFFECTIVELY IS something that I think a lot of jockeys struggle with. Actually, perhaps I should rephrase that to it being something that a lot of human beings struggle with. It's hard not to get carried away when you think something good is going to happen and it's hard not to get despondent when it doesn't. As is so often the way, the trick to managing your expectations effectively is finding a balance that doesn't upset your equilibrium too much. As a realist, and as somebody who doesn't allow themselves to get too carried away by success, I'm often quite good at managing my own expectations. What spoils it for me sometimes are the periods when I start to catastrophize. Ah well. Such is life.

With regards to the week ahead I have no such issues. The racing during the week is going to be quite poor as far as I'm concerned. I might stand a chance on a couple but I'm not likely to come away with very much at all. What's motivating me to keep going is the Jockeys Championship, of course, and the possibility that I might just be wrong. Nobody's forcing me to do it. It's a numbers game at the moment and will be until October. Sometimes I just have to take what's out there.

On Saturday it's the Derby. The quality will improve exponentially with regards to the horses, of course, but as far as my own chances are concerned, nothing much will change unfortunately. I'll be riding Bellum Justum for Andrew and he's a 20/1 outsider. I've just been having a look at the draw for the race and I'm in stall twelve next to Ancient Wisdom. The only horse I'd prefer to be a bit closer to is Los Angeles in four as following him would hopefully give me a nice lead and bring me into the race. After watching the final Ballydoyle gallops on social media a day or two ago, I was really taken with him. On good to firm ground he might lack a bit of pace on that track, but with the ground almost certainly being on the easy side of good, if not soft, I think he might win.

With regards to Bellum Justum, we have more questions than answers at the moment. He has actually won a trial on the Derby track but he's lazy in the morning and never goes past his work companions which makes it hard to get his heart rate up. I'd like to have ridden him out more in the lead-up to the Derby and pressed a few more buttons, but as well as potentially causing an injury it might have exposed him which could have put him off his feed. Yet again, it's all about finding a balance but in this case, and in cases like it, there are so many factors to consider. As a consequence, there will be horses going into the race that are under-prepared and also horses that are going in over-prepared. Bellum Justum is definitely not over-prepared, that's for sure. It wouldn't surprise me if he ran well but I think he'll stand more of a chance of success in the autumn.

I've been wracking my brains this morning trying to recall my earliest memory of the Derby. No particular race stands out from my childhood but one of the clearest memories from my teenage years is when Ryan Moore failed to win on Carlton House in 2011. He was the clear favourite that day and it was a huge shock to everyone. I remember Mickael Barzalona standing up in his irons in celebration as he came across the line on the winner, Pour Moi. Another strong memory is when Ruler Of The World won it in 2013. Once again, Ryan Moore was the pilot and the reason I remember it so clearly is because I'd ridden Ruler Of The World in some fast work as a two-year-old and I thought he was an aeroplane. A game changer for me as a spectator was when Camelot won it in 2012. I saw him almost daily while working at Ballydoyle and it brought the race to life. It was like discovering a new dimension.

There are also some Derbys I'd like to forget, such as when Serpentine went out in front in 2020 and didn't get caught. It's not the horses' fault, of course, but as a horse racing fan I want to see a proper race. A race in which some of the best horses in the world come into their own and compete. We saw that in 2023 with Auguste Rodin. I followed him on a horse called The Foxes that I've already mentioned and with a furlong or two to run he set off as though he'd just jumped in. The Derby is the one race where everyone in the racing world remembers who won the year before and it will always be recognized as one of the true championship races.

A few days ago, a racing fan asked me if there was any difference between the atmosphere in the weighing room prior to a big race such as the Derby and the atmosphere in there prior to a novices' race at Kempton or Newcastle. It's a good question. An outsider probably wouldn't notice any difference at all really, save for the fact that it might be a little bit quieter than normal. The banter still flows. It's what drives the banter that changes.

At an everyday race the banter could be driven by anything from the aforementioned STDs to the clothes that somebody's wearing. Taking the piss, mainly. Prior to a big race the banter will be more general, so we'll end up chatting about anything. If I had to describe the difference between the two in one word I'd say distracted. There's far more at stake before a big race and it's probably the one time when our thought streams will almost align.

I know I've already touched on how special I think the weighing room is but I've actually a bit more to say on the subject, as well as a few words about my return after the fourteen-month ban. My first race back was at Chelmsford and because it was considered to be newsworthy (at least by some sections of the media) there were a lot of photographers there and I even had to have security. None of that bothered me really. I was far more concerned about how my fellow jockeys might react.

Not being accepted in the weighing room would have been an incredibly hard cross to bear and I fully admit that it bothered me quite a bit prior to my return. Would I be welcomed back there or wouldn't I? In the end I needn't have worried. The moment I walked through the door, Kieran O'Neill started taking the rise out of me about the security and amount of photographers that were following me. He had a great big grin on his little face and I remember looking at him and thinking, *My God I've missed this*. To this day I don't think I've ever been as relieved to be mocked quite so mercilessly. It was exactly what I needed. Kieran's a good man.

Although I received a great deal of support when I resumed my racing career, from both the public and racing professionals alike, not everyone was happy to see me back. Not least certain members of the aforementioned press and media.

What appeared to infuriate them was that on my return I continued riding for the likes of Andrew and Sheikh Fahad, whereas in their eyes I should have been punished further by having to ride inferior horses for lesser-known trainers and owners. Then, when I started riding winners again, the reactions from these detractors went into overdrive and I became the subject of myriad discussions and rants. None of them positive or complimentary, unfortunately.

Although there was obviously a great deal of loyalty shown to me by the likes of Andrew and Sheikh Fahad, for which I will always be very grateful, the business we're in is results-driven and trainers are obliged to recommend a jockey who in their opinion will give their owner's horse or horses the best possible chance of winning. If that means hiring a jockey who is just coming back from a lengthy ban, so be it. There's nothing wrong with that, nor is it out of the ordinary. I had some serious issues, made several big mistakes, was punished accordingly and served my time.

Despite me not having raced for fourteen months, I had a good enough track record for many of the people who had employed me prior to the ban to continue doing so afterwards. And without wishing to blow my own trumpet, their decision was justified as I ended up riding 106 winners from May to October and finished second in the championship behind an incredibly in-form William Buick.

At first I thought that my critics must have been afflicted by something as they suddenly seemed incapable of grasping the fairly simple concept of an athlete receiving a ban for a transgression, serving said ban and then attempting to carry on with their life afterwards as best they can. For some reason these people wanted blood and some of the stuff they spouted and wrote was absolute bullshit. One or two well-known racing journalists and members of the panels on *ITV Racing* and *Luck on Sunday* in particular seemed almost disgusted that I was getting so many good rides and riding so many winners. One of them even complained that my murky past already appeared to have been forgotten about. Really?

The truth is that my past hadn't been forgotten then, the same as it hasn't been forgotten now. In fact, when I'm eventually called by God, should I be deemed worthy of having an obituary written about me in a newspaper, you can bet your bottom dollar that regardless of what I go on to achieve between now and then, my fourteen-month ban and my previous three-month ban for cocaine contamination will be referred to or mentioned in the headline and/or the opening paragraph.

'Oisin Murphy – former jockey who had success but was ultimately flawed.'

Am I OK with that? Actually, I am. After all, I won't be here to complain about it. What I am not OK with, however, is people within the racing industry – people who have some level of influence with the general public – putting somebody down when they're trying to pick themselves up and get their life back together again.

The effect that this had on me going forward was seismic, although I did learn a very valuable lesson. Before the ban

I would always go above and beyond in trying to help the press and media improve the experience of the racegoer by taking part in things like commentaries, race reviews and race previews. Frankie Dettori and Ryan Moore had always taken the opposite approach and prior to the ban I could never fully understand why. Now I understood perfectly. I still do the odd thing every now and then, but I'm very careful whom I say yes to.

I wasn't naive enough to believe that everybody would be happy to see me back in the saddle after serving my ban, but I'd rather hoped that this might be limited to a few idiotic trolls online. I was wrong, unfortunately.

In the interests of balance, I would like to mention one of two members of the press and media who have always treated me fairly. The journalist whom I have the most time for at the *Racing Post* is Peter Scargill. Jess Stafford from Racing TV has been amazing, as has Oli Bell at *ITV Racing*. The people at Sporting Life have been out of this world. In fact, they were the first ones to get in touch with me after the ban and they've always been very loyal. Emmet Kennedy too has been terrific.

I think one of the most switched-on racing presenters out there at the moment in terms of promoting the sport to a younger audience and utilizing social media effectively is Frankie Foster. He also speaks very well, has a bit of charisma and is genuinely interested. Racing needs more people like him in my opinion. A lot more.

Anyway, let's get back to the weighing room.

When I was an apprentice jockey, the elder statesmen of the weighing room were luminaries such as Richard Hughes, Jimmy Fortune and Kieren Fallon. Legends of the sport who had achieved everything at least twice over and who rightly commanded a commensurate amount of respect.

I remember feeling quite star-struck at first, that's for sure. Especially with Kieren. He was my first racing hero and I had posters of him on my wall. In fact, when Dylan Thomas won the Arc in 2017 with Kieren on board, that was when I decided I wanted to be a Flat jockey.

I found the weighing room to be quite hard going at first. I was considered by some jockeys to be a bit cocky in my early days, although at the time I had no idea why. I had very little belief in my own abilities and was constantly terrified. If I did appear cocky at all it was nothing more than a coping mechanism. My lifeblood back then was a hunger to succeed. If it hadn't been for that I'd have run a mile.

A far more tangible irritation for my fellow jockeys was the amount of success I had in my first two seasons. As somebody who was already considered to be a bit arrogant by some of my compatriots, this exacerbated the situation no end and for a while it made things uncomfortable. What got me through, as well as the will to succeed, was actually the confidence I gleaned from experiencing that success, although ironically it also got me into even more trouble.

To cut a long story short, I would sometimes make manoeuvres during races that were considered to be careless by some and when people took me to task over it, instead of just holding my hands up and apologizing I would defend myself and answer back. This eventually resulted in Martin Dwyer, Franny Norton and the top jockey coach George Baker grabbing me by the scruff of the neck, although fortunately not all at the same time.

I can't remember where Martin grabbed me but Franny

got hold of me at Chester one day and George at Kempton. The reasons for their complaints were all valid, I should say, and they were right to pull me up, literally! By attempting to put some manners on me, which I'm happy to say they did, Martin, Franny and George inadvertently helped me to appreciate the weighing room for what it is and I'll always be very grateful to them.

One of the most positive differences that exists between the weighing room now and the weighing room fifteen years ago is an almost tangible sense of empathy. Every jockey has problems and although we all vary as to how candid we are about our own, just the knowledge that you are among people who understand what you're going through can be an enormous strength.

An equally positive addition over recent years has been the increase in female jockeys. Hollie Doyle, Saffie Osborne, Hayley Turner, Joanna Mason and others. They're all great fun and have brought a new dimension to the atmosphere. They certainly don't take any crap from the blokes, that's for sure.

As much as I admire, respect and like my fellow jockeys, the main attraction in the weighing room for me person- ally are the valets. They are without question the unsung heroes of our profession and without them we wouldn't be able to function. They do everything for us. They maintain our equipment and our attire, assist us with our tack and keep the weighing room tidy. Valets are as important to a jockey as a coach is to a football team as without them noth- ing would work and everything would fall to pieces.

If you take into account how much time we spend in and around the weighing room (perhaps six or seven hours a day), jockeys probably spend more time with their valets than we do with our partners. Because it's so intense, the relationship between a jockey and a valet has to be looked after and that's something else that valets are extremely good at. They appreciate the amount of pressure we're under and know when to console us, when to celebrate with us and when to just leave us alone. They'll arrive at a track a good three hours before the first race and they'll be lucky to leave two hours after the last. They all work their socks off and are as adaptable as they are efficient and hard-working.

The three main valets I work with are David Mustow, John Edge and David Virco. David Mustow actually owns the company that employs David and John so there's never any conflict of interest. The three of them have been looking after me right from the beginning of my career so probably know me better than anyone else in the industry. They always know instinctively what my mood is like when I arrive and if they think I need cheering up they'll make me laugh. Even if I'm offhand with them, which I can be sometimes, they know it's just the pressure I'm under and would never take it to heart or judge me. They would literally do anything for me and I have an immeasurable amount of respect for all of them. The weighing room is a great place to be and valets are the beating heart of it.

THURSDAY, 13 JUNE 2024

Central London

If somebody had told me prior to going to Epsom that I'd come away from there with two wins, no hard luck stories in either the Oaks or the Derby and having avoided suspension, I'd have been happy enough. Fortunately, that's exactly what came to pass. Sure, I'd have liked to have done better in the big two, but I managed my expectations effectively and it paid dividends. A few years ago it might have been a different story but I'm a bit kinder to myself these days. The only real disappointment was Running Lion who went wrong in the Princess Elizabeth Stakes, but that's the nature of Epsom. She's by Roaring Lion who has probably been the most important horse in my career so far and I want her to do well.

I've got five races at Windsor this evening and am in London at the moment visiting various owners prior to Royal Ascot next week. I like coming up to London. It's such a contrast to where I live in Lambourn and there's a real buzz about the place.

What can I tell you about the build-up to Royal Ascot? Well, it starts coming into my consciousness in early March when I start to consider which horses might be suitable for the meeting and it builds up from there. By the middle of May, though, it's become an obsession. Like everything else really.

As with the Jockeys Championship, finding horses for Royal Ascot is also a numbers game as the majority of the candidates will fall by the wayside either due to injury or because they're simply not good enough. Other more promising candidates might fall by the wayside much closer to the meeting, which can be a real frustration. They can have the best preparation imaginable but then suddenly and inexplicably start coughing or something. It can happen at the drop of a hat. Another problem I've heard about recently is horses getting spots. It's a bit like eczema apparently and has been causing a lot of problems since early June. The trouble is that when you send off a sample from an infected horse to a vet, nothing's coming up. Or at least, nothing conclusive. It's a mystery. It's also very uncomfortable for the horses.

As worrying as things like this are for all concerned, for me personally I can do nothing at all about it so I just have to try and park the issue, redirect my attention and concentrate on the positives. With regards to Royal Ascot, one of the main positives for me this year comes in the shape of a gorgeous filly trained by David Menuisier called Tamfana that we believe might stand a chance in the Queen Elizabeth II Stakes. I had a run on her yesterday over at Chantilly and she felt good.

I've been quite up and down this last week. It's been a bit of an emotional roller coaster, due mainly to the fact that everything that could have happened has. I'm not explaining myself very concisely here, am I. I was at Sandown last Friday and Saturday and on paper it looked like I'd ride loads of winners. I didn't though. Not one. On a normal week that'd be bad enough for me but in the build-up to Royal Ascot . . . well, let's just say that I was a little bit emotional afterwards.

You might be thinking that, given what I've said several times already about managing my own expectations (not to mention the fact that I have counselling twice a week), episodes like this shouldn't really happen. If only. Contrary to what some people might believe, the aforementioned crutches are not a cure for an obsessive and/or unpredictable or anxious mind, just as periods of sobriety will not cure an alcoholic. If anything, they're like an early warning system. An internal radar that gives you the opportunity to respond thoughtfully to what might damage you, and in the case of my therapist an outlet for exploring and easing those thoughts. Is the system foolproof? Of course it isn't. What happened to me after Sandown is proof of that. After that meeting I started questioning my own ability and completely lost sight of reality. Everybody was asking me if I was looking forward to Royal Ascot and what my best rides were and I'd convinced myself that even if everything went right for me I might not be good enough. My lifeblood is and always has been winning, but the veins through which this lifeblood flows are all too often obstructed by pangs of self-doubt.

Incidentally, what drives all this isn't a particular condition or issue. I might well be a recovering alcoholic with an overactive mind, but first and foremost I am an athlete, an athlete who has an overwhelming desire to win everything I take part in. If I didn't have that desire I'd probably be fairly normal. Whatever normal is these days.

Despite the above I've actually been sleeping quite well just recently. I know, it's strange, isn't it. I might not have been able to persuade myself that I'm good enough to win races at Royal Ascot, which turned me upside down emotionally, but I was able to get some sleep. Not bad for somebody who is prone to bouts of insomnia.

I read in the declarations this morning that the field for the Commonwealth Cup which takes place later in the meeting has really cut up, with two of the most fancied runners having been ruled out. I wasn't down to ride either of those fortunately, but it just goes to show how quickly things change in this sport.

I reluctantly agreed to do a pre-Ascot interview with the

Racing Post a few days ago (against my better judgement) and, perhaps unsurprisingly, I'm already regretting it. The chap who conducted the interview, Peter Thomas, is great, but instead of leading with a racing headline (it was a pre-Ascot interview, after all), they decided to use something about my therapist instead. That was the first thing that pissed me off but a bit further down they quoted me as saying that Rob Hornby was silly to have got himself suspended, when what I was obviously referring to was the suspension itself (Rob was suspended for seven days because he forgot to weigh in on a horse that finished third). These are things that can get you into trouble with friends and acquaintances and I've had enough of it. Andrew Balding doesn't speak to the *Racing Post* at all and I can understand why. I don't think they go out of their way to piss people off and cause trouble but at the same time I don't think they do much to prevent it either.

Anyway, let's get back to Royal Ascot.

I appreciate that by the time you read this, the results will be obsolete but it still might be worthwhile going through each day and telling you what I fancy and why, just so you know what goes through the mind of a jockey prior to such a prestigious meeting.

The first race on the first day is the Queen Anne Stakes. Although I don't have a ride this year I'm interested by the fact that Inspiral isn't in there. A lot of punters will have had ante-post bets on Inspiral expecting her to run, so there'll be a lot of disappointed people. I think Roger Varian's horse, Charyn, with Silvestre de Sousa on board, has a great chance. For me, although he's 4/1, he would be the horse I'd most like to ride.

The second race is the Coventry Stakes which I won on Berkshire Shadow in 2021. My mount for this race is one of Joseph O'Brien's second string, a horse called Midnight Strike. It's a fair horse that won on debut and if I get the right trip I genuinely believe that he has what it takes to win a race like this. The ground worries me slightly as it might be too fast, but that's completely out of my control. All I know is that he'll be a much better horse with juice in the ground. What he achieved on debut at the Curragh wasn't normal and I'm happy to be partnering him. Saying that, there are at least ten horses in that race that I'd like to ride, but because they've only had one or two starts, it's difficult to choose the right one. Speaking of which, Andrew has one in there that I rode last time out (which was also his first time) called Cool Hoof Luke. Although I think he has a big future, I didn't think he'd be ready for a race like the Coventry and turned him down.

I have been asked on numerous occasions whether or not Andrew and I ever disagree about which horses I decide to ride, and to this day we've never come anywhere near. I'm not suggesting that disagreements would never take place between a trainer and a jockey in that scenario, but as well as trusting each other's judgement, Andrew and I are both fairly good at explaining ourselves and we always make a point of backing up a decision with a reason.

I've got a very good horse in the third race on the first day, the King Charles III Stakes. She's an Australian mare called Asfoora and her preparation has been pretty much perfect. We haven't looked under the bonnet as much as we'd have liked, but that's normal for Australian horses as they don't train them anywhere near as hard. Draw-wise, there's seventeen in there altogether and it could be one of those days when the draw makes all the difference. There's a fast horse two down from me called Regional that I'm hoping to get a tow from. The other fancied horses are all drawn really low so it's likely that the race will split into two halves. Because I'm on the stands side with Regional I just have to forget about the other horses, stick with him and ride my own race.

If I had to choose the horse that I'm most looking forward to riding at Royal Ascot it would have to be Middle Earth in the Hardwicke Stakes. There are one or two others in the race that could beat him such as Continuous and Desert Hero, but he's the one ride of the week that I wouldn't give up for anything.

I always get very moody in the run-up to Royal Ascot. Managing your expectations is all well and good, but sometimes you can't get over the fact that in some situations you're expected to win come what may, and Royal Ascot is a case in point. Not every race, of course, but the horses I tend to ride at Royal Ascot will often stand at least a chance of winning and the expectation is equal to that. I'd say the majority of jockeys will probably get a bit frazzled prior to Royal Ascot, just as a footballer might get a bit tense prior to a cup final.

On day two of the meeting I've got Wild Tiger for Saeed bin Suroor in the Royal Hunt Cup. He's handicapped (weighted) to win a race like this off 9 stone but he'll make his own luck because he can win on pace. I was very impressed with him at Goodwood last time out, despite the track not being ideal. He's bred to improve for going up to the mile and ran over seven furlongs last time out. In the Coronation Stakes I've got Ramatuelle, the French filly. She wasn't quite there in her coat on the first two starts this year and the jockey who rode her in the Qipco 1,000 Guineas last time out got a bit of stick for not winning, hence them putting me on. I don't know if she'll stay a mile but she's definitely the fastest horse in the race. I'll be trying to get her covered up.

I've actually just written a message to Ramatuelle's trainer, Christopher Head, giving him my opinion on where I think we stand and, more importantly, what my plan is for the race on Friday. This will give you an insight into how a jockey and trainer communicate, although I should point out that I don't do this before every race. It would be physically and mentally impossible.

CORONATION STAKES

I think Ryan [Moore] will stay out from 9 on Opera Singer and go forward. I expect him to probably lead. James [Doyle] will follow away on Elmalka. I don't think she'll be ridden as quietly as she was at Newmarket. Porta Fortuna will follow away. Tom Marquand will try and get behind Opera Singer. Rouhiya broke well in the Pouliches [Poule d'Essai des Pouliches – the French equivalent of the 1,000 Guineas]. I hope Maxime [Guyon] will try and sit close to Ryan. He's a smart jockey. I hope he will realize the tactics the favourite is likely to employ. Content will try and get in my way. See The Fire is working very well. I'm not sure what Andrew will tell [David] Probert. If I was riding her, I'd be trying to get close to James and Marquand.

Plan A – I want to take Ramatuelle down sleepy. She didn't charge the gate at Newmarket but I want to break a touch slow. I imagine myself following Maxime and I just

want to relax from the beginning and allow her to breathe
for the first half. She's the fastest horse in the race. If I
have a smooth trip and I don't give the others a head start,
hopefully I can sit and fill up before outsprinting them.

I suppose my other main chance at Royal Ascot this year will
be Michael Price and Michael Kent Jnr's horse Kitty Rose in
the Sandringham Stakes. Her form is on soft ground in Ireland. I only cantered her at Newmarket last week and she felt
like an absolute aeroplane. It's not a great race though so I
won't get too excited. I have at least one winning chance for
every day of the meeting which is all you can really wish for.

Another positive during Royal Ascot is that it's not too
taxing work-wise. The races start quite early compared to what
I'm used to and I'll be home at a decent hour for a change. I'll
still be riding out most mornings but that'll settle my nerves a
bit and give me something else to concentrate on.

There is one last thing I'd like to tell you about before I go. I
was actually in two minds whether to do so after it happened
(you'll understand why in a moment), but in the interests of
being honest and giving you a warts-and-all account of what
it's like being a jockey, I thought to hell with it.

On the way back from a race meeting last week I suddenly
felt quite ill but before I could ask my driver to stop the car,
I began to projectile vomit. The only saving grace was that
I was sitting in the back of the car and not the front, otherwise there could have been an accident. The doctor said
that it might have been E. coli, which was slightly alarming.
Because we eat so little we're probably a lot more susceptible
to bugs and things. That alone should be reason enough not

to pursue such a profession but we do it anyway. Ah well. It's all character-building.

By the way, because it's Royal Ascot I'm going to try and do an entry for each day of the meeting, although depending on how I get on they might be quite short. Let's hope that's not the case.

TUESDAY, 18 JUNE 2024

Lambourn

I'm in bed now after what has been a fairy tale of a day. I was hopeful that Asfoora might do well in the Group 1 but she exceeded my expectations to such an extent that I was able to take a deep breath at the end and enjoy it. It was an incredible feeling. I said the other day that we weren't quite sure how strong she might be because we hadn't pressed enough buttons, but she had plenty in the tank and some to spare.

The ride was offered to me after I won on a horse at York a few weeks ago called Jubilee Walk. When the owners got in touch I jumped at the chance. It's one of the best decisions I've made in quite a while. Apart from Asfoora, I rode nothing that finished in the first three today, but I'm certainly not complaining. Everything ran as expected and I did everything I could so there were no shocks or disappointments.

It's going to be tough tomorrow. I have Wild Tiger in the Royal Hunt Cup. He's favourite and is the right type of horse so I know I chose well. The only thing that worries me slightly is the ground being too fast for him. Anyway, that obviously fits into the 'cannot do a damn thing about it' category, so I'll be quiet and talk about something else.

The atmosphere at the track today was amazing. It usually is at Royal Ascot but I got the feeling that everyone was just really happy to be there. I suppose it's the same every year but by the time it comes around again it's been long enough to give you a nice little surprise.

I thought the applause that Asfoora and I received after our win was a bit muted which is understandable really as she's unknown. This was more than compensated for by a group of Australian racegoers who I'd hazard a guess had been on it since breakfast time.

The main noticeable absentee at this year's meeting is, of course, the great Frankie Dettori, somebody who I feel very honoured to be able to call my friend. I think he's here doing some media, but not to have him in the weighing room feels very strange indeed.

Frankie's mere presence at Royal Ascot became known as the 'Frankie Factor' and his name is still synonymous, not just with the meeting but, thanks to heroics such as his 'Magnificent Seven' during the British Festival of Racing in 1996, the track itself. In fact, I'd go as far as to say that Frankie Dettori is the only jockey since Lester Piggott or Willie Carson who transcends the sport of horse racing and he continues to be a great ambassador.

Frankie used to come alive at Royal Ascot and when you think about the meeting, he's the first jockey that comes to mind. In 2021 I just pipped him to leading rider with six winners each, but I had more placings. As somebody who had always admired Frankie and wanted to emulate his success, it was an absolute dream come true. And who was the first person to congratulate me when it happened? He was. Frankie is an outrageously competitive human being but I think he knew that my happiness at beating him that year was the biggest compliment I could pay him. It was the ultimate accolade for me.

Frankie used to arrive in a top hat and tails to Royal Ascot which, given his standing there, always seemed perfectly normal. I actually copied him one year, as did Olivier Peslier. He and Ryan Moore used to travel to the meeting by helicopter each day, which was very flash. All I could think about on seeing them was how much their expenses must have been without even riding a winner.

The first time I met Frankie, his career was in the doldrums. He'd only recently returned from a six-month ban and was riding an outsider on the all-weather at Lingfield. He wasn't in great shape and was a far cry from the Frankie of old whom I'd watched and admired on television on probably hundreds of occasions.

Over the next couple of weeks I saw Frankie occasionally either in the sauna or in the weighing room, and the general consensus among members of the press and race-going public and professionals was that his career was probably over. Then, out of nowhere, he managed to get himself a job as a retained rider for Sheikh Joaan Al Thani's Al Shaqab Racing. Regular trips to France soon followed and all of a sudden he was busy again and riding decent horses. Most of all, he was hungry.

This all led to John Gosden knocking on Frankie's door which, after then going on to win the Derby for him on Golden Horn as well as the Prix de l'Arc de Triomphe and the Oaks on Enable, confirmed his status as one of British sport's true renaissance men.

I've been aware of Frankie Dettori for almost as long as I can remember. He and Kieren Fallon were my two big heroes as a kid, although Frankie's personality probably resulted in him spending more time in my consciousness. Subsequently, I ended up naming one of our dogs after him. Frankie was winning everything at the time and it seemed to make sense. We lived in the countryside and the dog kept on going missing. Then he'd come back when he was hungry and I'd play with him for a couple of hours and he'd disappear again looking for female dogs. To be honest with you he was a nightmare.

My memories of Frankie over the last eight or nine years (that's the jockey, not the dog) are of him sitting at the very top of world racing and being the go-to jockey when a top ride became available. That's in addition to winning Classics and Group races for John Gosden and Sheikh Joaan Al Thani, of course. If anything, Frankie became even more determined during his resurgence and even more professional. He never messed up and always made the best of his opportunities. Agents can book you plenty of rides, but Frankie was always looking at which horses might be entered into which races and who might or might not be available to ride them, positioning himself accordingly. People often talk about Lester Piggott's ability to take advantage of this kind of thing, but Frankie was right up there with him.

The reason I mention it is because Frankie was nearly always the jockey who would step in for me when I couldn't partner a horse in a big race, and nine times out of ten he'd be successful. Had that been any other jockey I dare say I might have become a bit resentful after a while, but Frankie Dettori stepping in for me felt more like a privilege. It's like

Lewis Hamilton offering to give your mum a lift to the shops because you're stuck at work. The man's a superstar.

I've actually been on holiday with Frankie a few times, most memorably to Barbados a few years ago. He constantly took the piss out of me for being overweight, which was entertaining. He's a very good swimmer is Frankie and I made the stupid mistake one day of forgetting to tell him that I was anything but. We were out jet skiing and for a laugh I deliberately drove my jet ski into his which sent him flying into the water. In hindsight this was not one of my best ideas. As well as not being able to swim I had no lifejacket on and we must have been about a mile and a half out to sea. Worse still, I had just knocked into the water a mad Italian who, when I informed him that I couldn't swim, didn't seem too bothered about it. All he wanted was revenge and he soon returned the favour. I ended up about fifteen feet away from my jet ski and without any help from him I managed to doggy paddle my way back and drag myself back on board. It was all my own fault, of course, and he thought it was hilarious.

In the weighing room, Frankie was almost always in a good mood. He was only showing up two or three days a week and usually for a good reason. He could be very loud when he'd had a good day but when he'd been beaten on three or four favourites he could be very quiet. On the whole though, he was an absolute joy to be around.

I was asked by a TV presenter at the track earlier today whether or not I could see myself taking Frankie's place at Royal Ascot, and my answer was an emphatic no. Nobody could replace Frankie Dettori, least of all me. I have the same will to win as he does but I don't have the confidence or charisma. As I said before, Frankie transcends the sport of horse racing and is probably its only breakout star at the moment. Not everybody knows what Frankie Dettori has achieved over the years but everyone knows who he is. He's a household name, not just here in the UK but all over the world. He also has a very thick skin which is exactly what you need if you're going to be that famous and not let it affect you.

Fortunately, Frankie loves FaceTiming people and I have the pleasure of seeing and speaking to him regularly, or whenever he's bored which is basically all the time. First of all he'll complain about the weather for a bit over in Kentucky or New York and then he'll complain about everything else. Never mind about how bad my week's going! I'm like his therapist. It's something I always look forward to, though.

Anyway, I've got six or seven two-year-olds to ride out tomorrow morning before I go to Ascot so I'd better get some sleep. It's been a really good day.

THURSDAY, 20 JUNE 2024

Lambourn – 8am

I'm just on my way to ride out for a small trainer from Monmouthshire called Tom Faulkner. He used to be a point-to-point rider before becoming a trainer and he has a decent horse that he's bringing all the way down to the gallops here in Lambourn for me to ride.

Unfortunately, I didn't get time to record an entry yesterday as by the time I got home I was completely whacked. I'm pleased to report though that once again it was an absolute fairy tale of a day, despite the first race going badly. I had the favourite in that race (one of Andrew's called Kassaya) and we were in traffic for the full five furlongs. I never got the chance to let go of her head which was incredibly frustrating. My ride in the second race, Mina Rashid, ran as expected (slowly) and then came the first of two winners: Running Lion in the Duke of Cambridge Stakes followed by Wild Tiger in the Royal Hunt Cup. These two were very special. Running Lion because he's owned by David Howden who is very good to me and Wild Tiger because he's trained by Saeed bin Suroor who, after Andrew, is my most loyal trainer. That makes it three for me so far. I'd have taken that at the start of the week, that's for sure.

Today's going to be a bit tougher, I think. And that's not just me being negative. I've got Tropical Storm in the Norfolk Stakes who I think might stand a chance. Warda Jamila in the George V Stakes is less likely to thrive, although you never know. Kalpana in the Ribblesdale will be the favourite but she's tough although I'm worried about fast ground. After that I've got Coltrane in the Gold Cup who's a legend but is not getting any younger. He'll need to start well to stand any chance. That's the problem with winning, you see. If it's feeding an addiction, which it normally is, you're always desperate for more.

Incidentally, it was wonderful to see a post on social media today from the Prince and Princess of Wales congratulating Ryan Moore and Aidan O'Brien on their success in the Prince of Wales's Stakes. The patronage by the Royal Family of British racing continues to be a huge stamp of approval for the sport. As does the involvement of the Royal Families of Saudi Arabia, Kuwait, Dubai, Abu Dhabi, Bahrain and Qatar.

In terms of the British Royal Family, racing is the only major sport that they're involved in commercially which sets us apart from all the others. A member of the family might attend Wimbledon or the FA Cup final but the fact that the ruling British monarch will always attend every day of Royal Ascot is something to be proud of. Things might have changed in the world but horse racing is still the sport of Kings.

THURSDAY, 20 JUNE 2024

Lambourn – 11pm

Today has been a strange one, that's for sure. In fact, I'm not sure how I'm going to describe it without sounding like a bit of a lunatic. The morning went OK but then as soon as I got to Ascot everything seemed to happen in slow motion. It might have had something to do with a lack of food but it felt very bizarre. Most importantly, it didn't affect what I did in the saddle. I rode as well as I could and there were no hard luck stories. Most of the horses I rode today ran career bests but there were no nice surprises, just as I feared. They simply weren't good enough.

The King Power horse, Bellum Justum, ran better than he did in the Derby and finished third. I was very happy to lead on him as I know he saves plenty of energy, but on this occasion he had nothing left in the final furlong. It could have been the ground but that spark of energy that he had on his start at Epsom wasn't there and I had to ask him to switch leads. The other King Power horse, Mission To Moon, ran a career best to be fourth in the Britannia.

Andrew is having a tough meeting so far. He must have had more placed runners than any other trainer bar Aidan O'Brien, but no winners. I really do hope he can get on the scoresheet as he deserves some success.

Now might be a good time for me to go into detail about my relationship with Andrew. He'll hate me for doing it, but he's played such a pivotal role in my development both as a jockey and as a human being that it would be remiss and disrespectful of me not to write a few words.

Andrew's quite a shy person and when I first arrived at Kingsclere all those years ago he had a lot of apprentices and I wasn't sure if a relationship would develop. As I've said, there were ten of us there and they all looked better on a racehorse than I did. That isn't false modesty. It's a fact. I did, however, make an effort to learn the pedigrees of the horses and I could see when coming back from the gallops that Andrew appreciated that I had some knowledge as well as an opinion or two of my own. I tried not to get too enthusiastic or go into too much detail as I didn't want to sound cocky, but I worked hard to get to know the horses in the yard and be informed about what was going on.

I'd only been there a couple of months before I was sent on my apprentice course, which was apparently quite rare back then, particularly at Kingsclere. The first ride that Andrew gave me was on a horse called Imperial Glance at Salisbury. A fortnight before, he pulled me to one side, told me I'd got the ride and said that he would win, and we did. As a confidence boost that was massive. Being an apprentice to a trainer of Andrew's stature was obviously a big thing for an aspiring jockey but for him to then put me on a favourite was a huge step up. Success is the number one reason why we do what we do but a nod from someone you admire a great deal is very nearly as gratifying. One feeds the other I suppose. Andrew could easily have put any one of the other nine apprentices on that horse and I wouldn't have felt aggrieved. He didn't, though, and that was the start of what has been, and what I hope will continue to be, a very fruitful relationship.

Andrew's always been very fair with me. If he's unhappy with a ride – which thankfully hasn't happened in recent years, and long may that continue – as an apprentice and a professional he would always tell me why he was disappointed and then explain what I should have done. After that it was always forgotten about and was never mentioned again. That really helped me to take things one race at a time which, when you're starting out, is incredibly important in my opinion. Obviously you have to learn from your mistakes but you take what you need and then you leave the rest behind. I have huge respect for Andrew for doing that.

When I first arrived at Kingsclere in October 2012, Andrew had approximately ninety horses. He's now taken that number up to over 250. That in itself is remarkable, but what it's also done is allow Andrew and his wife Anna Lisa to invest in the facilities and turn Kingsclere into an outstanding world-class training establishment.

With regards to our relationship now, Andrew and I attend award ceremonies together occasionally and we also travel together once in a while. He's a bit of a home bird, though, so Anna Lisa will often do the foreign trips. If we're at a meeting together, she and I will often sit down and have a meal and a laugh together which is nice. As well as being incredibly bright, Anna Lisa is a very warm human being and she took wonderful care of me when I first moved over to England.

With Andrew it's a bit different. He obviously has an awful lot on his plate with everything that's going on and so we don't really socialize. Besides, we have to have room to breathe and if we were seeing each other outside of work as well it would probably become a case of familiarity breeding contempt. He's also an avid supporter of Southampton FC, which in itself precludes me from even acknowledging him outside of working hours. As a Chelsea fan I could never lower myself.

Until fairly recently we didn't even text each other very much, but now when I'm away in, say, Japan or Hong Kong, he'll touch base from time to time and ask me how I'm finding it or congratulate me on a winner. My professional relationship with Andrew is one of the ones that I'd like to last until the end of my career. I've always been extremely content riding for him and am conscious that I should always give him my best, day in, day out. It's almost like having a favourite teacher at school. The teachers whom you liked and who encouraged you the most were always the ones you wanted to do well for.

Getting on with Andrew's owners is obviously very important to me but I don't have to make much effort as they're all very nice people. It's the same with the team at Kingsclere. If the main stable jockey arrives in a bad mood driving a fancy car, then the people who are there doing all the hard work will not consider them to be part of the team. Not only could that create a bad atmosphere but it could also have a detrimental effect on the yard's form. After all, why should they put in the hard work for somebody who doesn't appreciate their efforts? First and foremost, the team at Kingsclere are good people so why on earth wouldn't you want to get on with them? Hopefully they appreciate the fact that I appreciate them.

While I was having my difficulties with alcohol, Andrew never once put his foot down and threatened to get rid of me. He'd have been perfectly within his rights to do so and for all manner of reasons, but he didn't. Not once. He's always been very supportive and the only questions he ever asked me, either after I'd been charged or during the ban, were about what he and Anna Lisa could do to help.

I remember him saying to me one morning after it all came out that I was still part of the team. I felt very alone at the time and being reminded of the fact that actually I wasn't was a great tonic. During the suspension Andrew went out of his way, not only to keep me occupied by allowing me to ride out for him, but by motivating me and always making sure I had something to look forward to. 'Don't forget about what you're going to ride when you're back,' he'd say to me. He'd then reel off the names of all his best horses and what he hoped we'd achieve together. I felt included in everything and he made me feel like I had a place within the team and, most importantly with regards to my recovery, a purpose. This not only helped me get back on the straight and narrow, but it motivated me to come back even stronger, which I actually think I have. That's in no small part down to Andrew Balding. He is the best of us and I will always be very grateful to him, to Anna Lisa and to the entire Kingsclere team.

SATURDAY, 22 JUNE 2024

En route to Park House Racing, Kingsclere

It's ten past five in the morning and I'm on my way to Andrew's to ride out two two-year-olds, Royal Playwright and New Endeavour. With regards to the last couple of days, there were no great surprises or excuses and the majority of my horses ran career bests, including Tropical Storm who finished second on Thursday. It was frustrating yesterday to hit the crossbar with Ramatuelle as well, but there we go. She relaxed brilliantly for me but the stiff mile may have caught her out. I can't say for sure as this was my first time on her, but I have a sneaking suspicion that her experiences in the Qipco 1,000 Guineas might have had an effect and she's still tired.

Today could be tough again, particularly for Andrew, but we'll keep trying. My immediate concern when I'm not winning is my position in the championship, whereas for a trainer it'll be the reaction of the owners, not to mention the small matter of keeping a business going. As daunting as my own dilemma can be sometimes, I wouldn't like to swap places with Andrew. Not for the world. Then again, nearly all his horses have been running to the best of their ability which means he's fulfilling his side of the bargain. Hopefully that will drive his owners to get better horses and go again next year.

MONDAY, 24 JUNE 2024

Lambourn

You'd be forgiven for assuming that after the madness of Royal Ascot I might just have allowed myself some time off for good behaviour. After all, four winners including two Group 1s isn't a bad return, even for a pessimistic realist like me. If that is what you were assuming, you'd be absolutely right as on Sunday morning I got on a plane to Athens where Sheikh Fahad had rented a 29-metre-long yacht. I spent Sunday evening on the yacht, which was very nice indeed, and after messing around in the water for an hour or two on Monday morning, I ate a fried egg and flew back to Heathrow. A car then picked me up and took me to Windsor for six rides and I walked away with two more winners. I was also up at 5.30 this morning to ride six pieces of work for David Menuisier including Sunway and some two-year-olds. Sunway's going to run in the Irish Derby on Sunday and today was the best he's ever felt. He is about 100/1 for the Irish Derby this morning but I think he'll go well.

Anyway, I can't hang about. I've got five to ride at Newbury later on today and will be at Andrew's first thing tomorrow riding out before visiting the dentist, having a therapy session and then lunch with Neville Bilpodiwala followed by five more at Kempton. One of these days I might stop and take a breath. Just not yet.

FRIDAY, 28 JUNE 2024

En route to Doncaster Racecourse

I've been feeling very down this past couple of days. Just really flat and lethargic. Unless it's something obvious that I can attend to immediately it's best not to overthink the reasons why, although if I were to hazard a guess I'd say it was down to the championship and the fact that my strike rate isn't where I'd like it to be. Either that or it's just post Royal Ascot blues. Win or lose, the energy at Royal Ascot is almost palpable and it carries you on. The wasting thing can be a bastard sometimes but I don't think it's that. Because it's been a part of my life for so long I know when it's becoming a problem and will try and bat it away. The championship is also with me twenty-four hours a day, but unlike the wasting I can't just put it to one side. I only wish I could.

The thing I find most difficult when I'm feeling like this is keeping a civil tongue in my head. I always try my best to be patient and polite (it's how I was brought up) but when this kind of gloom is upon me I tend to snap at the slightest thing. I certainly don't mean to. It's just what happens. The good thing is I'm aware of it and I always apologize.

Somebody I've already mentioned quite a lot in the book is Sheikh Fahad who is the chairman of Qatar Racing. As with Andrew, he is somebody with whom I have a very close working relationship. Andrew is the trainer who employs me the most often and Sheikh Fahad is the owner I ride for most frequently.

The first time I met Sheikh Fahad was at the Qipco British

Champions Day at Ascot in 2013. The last race on the card used to be an apprentice handicap and I'd been booked to ride one of Hugo Palmer's well in advance. When the entries came out, Andrew called me into the office. 'You're going to have to get off Palmer's horse,' he said to me. 'OK, but why?' I asked. 'You have to ride the Qatar horse instead.' I remember being a bit taken aback when he said that but at the same time I was obviously excited. It was a big deal riding for such a large and prestigious organization, especially as an apprentice.

The horse in question was called Dubawi Sound and it ran in Pearl Bloodstock colours which are yellow with blue stars. It ran badly, I remember, but Sheikh Fahad was understanding and very kind and complimentary. He was a real gent.

The following spring I started riding a few of Qatar's third-string horses when Jamie Spencer and Harry Bentley weren't available, and I ended up winning the Temple Stakes at Haydock for them on a horse called Hot Streak trained by Irishman Kevin Ryan, which was by Iffraaj. As the Temple Stakes is a Group 2 race, that was obviously a very big deal for a young jockey, but the fact that it brought me closer to the attentions of Sheikh Fahad and Qatar Racing made it even more exciting.

A couple of months later in the summer of that year, I was invited to have dinner with Sheikh Fahad for the first time. To say I was nervous would be a gross understatement. The restaurant was just off Park Lane in London so very exclusive and I can only really compare it to walking into Ballydoyle or Kingsclere for the first time. Just thinking about it makes the hairs on the back of my neck stand on end.

During the dinner, Sheikh Fahad told me that Qatar

Racing were interested in me riding for them regularly and asked if I would be open to that. Internally, I almost exploded, but outwardly I just smiled and muttered something along the lines of, 'Really, that'd be nice.' I came away from the restaurant on a cloud of euphoria. It was an amazing feeling. For a start, Sheikh Fahad and I seemed to get on very well which was important, but I was also just nineteen years of age and had been a jockey for less than sixteen months. To be guaranteed so many quality rides so early in my career was off the scale.

When I started riding for Qatar regularly, I was over at Newmarket almost every week, and in addition to us travelling to the races together, Sheikh Fahad insisted that I stay at his house. I remember driving his Ferrari into John Gosden's yard one morning at about 6am and parking it in the ring next to the likes of Frankie Dettori, Paul Hanagan and Rab Havlin. The looks they gave me were hilarious. It was as if they were saying, who the hell's this flash idiot?

The crux of my professional relationship with Sheikh Fahad is the same as my relationship with Andrew and Gavin which is trust, honesty, loyalty and respect. For instance, when I feel like I should have done something differently on a horse, which happens sometimes, I'll always be upfront and tell him. Not just because I always want to be honest, but because the ensuing discussion will often bear fruit. And it works both ways. If Sheikh Fahad feels like I could have done something differently on a horse, as opposed to just telling me after the race and having a go at me, we'll have a civilized discussion and try and take something from it. Also, if Sheikh Fahad ever feels like I'm not the right jockey for a horse and I get passed over, there's never any resentment. I always believe that whatever decision is made is always for the greater good.

As with the likes of Andrew and Gavin, because of my transgressions over the years, Sheikh Fahad could easily have dropped me several times, but he's always been completely loyal. I've been able to repay some of that loyalty by riding winners for him and the fact that we've had so much success together is a source of great joy. Last year we had only one Group 1 with New Century, but we had so many good days with the likes of Middle Earth and Queen Of The Pride. We always operate at a high strike rate together and that means the world to me.

MONDAY, 8 JULY 2024

Lambourn

I wasn't planning to record another entry until later on in the week, but this weekend has been quite eventful so I thought I'd better get it down before I forget the details. Have I mentioned I have an awful memory? When I'm as busy as I am at the moment it gets even worse.

Friday was one of the most difficult days I've had in months. I had six rides at Sandown and came away with five seconds and one third. The word demoralized doesn't really do justice to how I was feeling when I left the track. I felt like retiring. Although only for a minute or two.

Sandown has actually been a graveyard for me this year, but because I'd been in such good form all week I'd forgotten about that. Also, all but one of my rides at Sandown stood more than a fighting chance, so when we pulled up at the track I had a smile on my face and was looking forward to the day. Realistically, I thought I'd come away with two winners which would have kept my strike rate at roughly 22 per cent which is where it needs to be if I'm going to keep my lead and win the championship.

First up was a Listed race for two-year-olds and my horse, a filly called It Ain't Two for Hugo Palmer, was joint third favourite. Although she was always in touch with the leader and eventual winner, one of Archie Watson's horses with James Doyle on board called Aesterius, she didn't have quite enough and they ended up pulling clear of us with just under a furlong to go. No matter. If anything my horse had exceeded expectations so my confidence was intact. My time would come, either in the next race or the one after. I was sure of it.

My mount in the second race, called Existent, was second favourite. He hadn't run since September 2023 so was a bit of an unknown quantity. After almost falling out of the stalls we got held up at the rear for most of the race, although he ran on well in the final furlong to snatch second. This is when I started to smell a rat. I'm not a suspicious person but you just know when it isn't going to be your day.

Sure enough, the next three races were all variations of what had taken place before and my God, it was frustrating. Halfway through the sixth and final race of the day, I genuinely believed that my luck was about to change. My horse, Whispering Royal, normally looks quite slow, but after a steady start I got him to run hands and heels going forward. Here we go, I thought. At last. We could win this. But you know how stiff Sandown is. In the final furlong, even before I used my stick, he gave up the ghost just like that. The only consolation was that we finished third instead of second. It obviously felt counter-intuitive hoping that we'd finish further down the field, but having the words 'six seconds in a row at Sandown' etched on to my consciousness for all eternity would not have been pleasant. For sure, five was bad enough.

Because of traffic it took us over three hours to get home, which afforded me the unwelcome luxury of having plenty of time to contemplate what had taken place. Fortunately, I had the small matter of five races at Haydock the following day to distract me, including the Lancashire Oaks and the Old Newton Cup Handicap. Not to mention the German Derby on Sunday. As much as I talk about things like this affecting me, and they do, the fact of the matter is I'm still here. Still breathing and still fighting.

After another three-hour-plus drive up to Haydock, which was nice, Saturday's meeting got off to an inauspicious start when my mount in the first race ran badly, finishing fourth. Then, in race two, which was a one-mile-six-furlong handicap, my horse, Wild Waves, slipped on the home bend, as did the favourite Dramatic Star with Tom Marquand on board and Games People Play with Rossa Ryan. When things like that happen, which they do from time to time, it can be terribly conflicting. I actually saw Tom slip right in front of me. Half of me was thinking about my own race – 'damn, he's affected my momentum' – and the other half was thinking about him – 'I hope he's still standing'. Instinctively, I took a quick look over my shoulder to make sure he was still up, which he was, thank God. But then the job in hand kicked in again demanding my full and undivided attention. I shook my reins, asking for more, but just two strides later my horse tripped and I began saying a Hail Mary to myself, just as I had done at Windsor in May on He's Got Game. Fortunately, we all made it over the line safely but it had been a concussion and a broken collarbone waiting to happen. Not just for me but for all of us.

A week or two ago, the Clerk of the course at Haydock had been criticized by the press and by various industry people about watering, but because rain had been forecast the night before they didn't bother. Unfortunately, the forecast was incorrect and the rain didn't materialize which wasn't their fault. As a result, the track in the straight and the bend where we were racing on fresh ground was good to firm and it very nearly ended in disaster. In fact, had all three of us gone down I dread to think what might have happened. It would have been carnage.

After that they slit the track and sanded it which they hoped would do the trick, and after a fairly long inspection and a twenty-five-minute delay, the next race, which was the Lancashire Oaks, was allowed to go ahead. Notwithstanding the fact that the Lancashire Oaks is a Group 2, we all had one eye on the ground throughout the race. Sure enough, as we came around the home bend, the favourite, Tiffany, with Luke Morris on board, slipped, just as we three had done before. I was running just behind him on Queen Of The Pride for John and Thady Gosden and at that moment I had an awful feeling that more might quickly follow. Fortunately, on this occasion I was wrong. All eight of us made it home safely but the appetite to continue racing had waned significantly.

Queen Of The Pride and I went on to win the race after just pipping Tiffany to the post. I can't tell you how much the trip had affected that horse's performance (only Luke could tell you that), but after yet another inspection, the final three races of the afternoon were abandoned due to unsafe ground, including the £150,000 Old Newton Cup Handicap. As I'm sure you can imagine, there were a lot of very disappointed racegoers after the announcement, but as somebody who had experienced first-hand the reason why the races couldn't go ahead, the only emotion I felt as I left the track was relief.

On Sunday I had to be up at the crack of dawn for a six-and-a-half-hour, three-leg journey from Lambourn to Hamburg for the German Derby. It was a car from Lambourn to Stansted followed by a Ryanair flight to Hamburg and then a car from Hamburg Airport to Galopprennbahn Hamburg-Horn. I actually don't mind this kind of journey as you've got a nice bit of variety and are able to do some serious people watching. If that were a sport I'd be Olympic standard, no question about it.

The German Derby often clashes with good racing in places like France, but not this year. So, when I was asked to partner the favourite for the race a couple of weeks ago (a horse called Wintertraum trained by Waldemar Hickst in Cologne), I said yes immediately. It's a big ride. Wintertraum had also won three of his last four races and likes juice in the ground which they have plenty of over there.

As opposed to following my instinct during the race, I decided to stick to my original plan and this time it worked against us. I always have an idea prior to a race about how I should ride based on factors such as the field, where I'm drawn and the ground. And the trainer will have theirs, of course. Nine times out of ten I'll go my own way (it's always my choice and I take full responsibility if it goes wrong), but depending on what happens I might alter what I do. I was in two minds on this occasion and unfortunately I made the wrong choice. We thought the pace was going to be strong but it wasn't, and as opposed to sitting behind the leaders, which was the original plan, I should have followed my instinct and moved. As it was, because of the pace I found it impossible to get into the race and by the time we got into the straight (it's just two furlongs to the finish line) I had a mountain to climb.

On a lighter note, the winning jockey of the German Derby, Thore Hammer Hansen, is somewhat unique in that he's a German jockey with a German passport who speaks fluent English but with a broad Irish accent. He was an apprentice with Richard Hannon who always has a lot of Irish staff working for him, so when it came to Thore picking up English, it came with an Irish lilt. Honestly, from speaking to him you'd think he was from the same town as me.

SATURDAY, 13 JULY 2024

Lambourn

The frustrations of finishing second on multiple occasions are fortunately offset sometimes by a nice run of winners and over the past week or so I've had more than my fair share. As with the run of seconds, the secret is not to get too carried away by what's happening and to treat every race as a fresh start. A fresh opportunity. As with most things, that's far easier said than done, but you're far more likely to achieve it after a win or two than you are a string of seconds. It's not an exact science though, at least for me.

Although I appreciate the importance of enjoying the good times when they happen, I sometimes forget to make room for them in my head which does me no favours whatsoever. My default position as an unnaturally competitive athlete who could worry for Ireland is to attempt to negate whatever might go wrong in the future and if I can't negate it I'll fret about it. For instance, what's going through my head at this very moment in time is that I've ridden fifty-five more races than anyone else in the last two months and nobody I know rides out as much as I do. Even so, William Buick could easily ride four winners at Newmarket today and Tom Marquand could ride three. The only thing I can do to prevent that from having an effect on my lead in the championship is to carry on doing more than everyone else.

Let me give you another example.

By the time I arrived at Newmarket on Thursday for the July meeting I had four wins to my name since Monday, not to mention a healthy lead in the championship. I'd also been sleeping quite well, wasting hadn't been too much of a problem and I was full of confidence. The thing is, instead of just enjoying all this while it lasted, on Wednesday night I started fixating on a series of negatives regarding Newmarket, such as the distance you have to travel from the parade ring to the start. It's almost like riding in a pre-race race. The horses are fighting you sometimes, you're fighting them, and all you want is for them to relax and walk slowly. It can be exhausting, especially if there are a handful of races that are a mile or a mile and a quarter.

On Thursday there were seven races on the card and by the time we got to the penultimate race I was physically and mentally exhausted. So much so that if somebody had given me an excuse to leave the course there and then, I might well have taken it. I then ended up winning the last race on a horse called Sterling Night that we didn't think stood a chance and I spent an hour or two afterwards beating myself up for having wanted to leave. Not allowing enough room in my head for the things that go right in my life and concentrating too much on what can potentially go wrong is something else that leaves me frazzled and feeling lethargic. I can be my own worst enemy sometimes.

Later on that evening I took stock of what had happened, not just at Newmarket but the whole week. I came to the conclusion (and surprisingly quickly for me) that my week had been fairly good so far and appreciating the fact wouldn't harm my chances of doing it all again. I keep on claiming to be a realist and the reality of the situation was that I'd had a good week and it was only Thursday evening.

On Friday I woke up feeling a hundred times better and had two more wins at Newmarket making it nine for the week so far with a day to go. Last time I was at Newmarket for more than one day I had one winner from ten or eleven rides so it's a good return. Normally my first thought on waking up would be how my fellow championship contenders might get on today, but instead I'm trying to focus on the fact that I'll be riding three favourites at Ascot before jumping on a plane to Longchamp to ride Tamfana for David Menuisier in the Grand Prix de Paris. I have to make 8st 9lb for that. Although I've been very cautious about what I've been consuming these past two days, I wanted to eat something this morning as a couple of those horses are going to take some riding. I had two fried eggs and half a glass of water, but all of a sudden I've gone from 8st 9lb and a quarter to 8st 10lb and a half, so when I finish this entry I'll be getting straight in the bath.

There's been a lot of talk recently about Dido Harding becoming the senior steward at the Jockey Club. One or two people have asked me for my opinion on the appointment and the truth is that I don't really have one. Not because I'm not interested. It's because there's been no positive change within the British horse racing industry for a very long time, and appointments such as these are usually down to tokenism or nepotism. It's the same as a general election. People get their hopes up but are ultimately disappointed. *Plus ça change*.

You're not going to believe this but tomorrow I've decided to put myself first for a change and take a whole day off. Hughie Morrison was going to run a filly at Chantilly that's a half-sister to Telecaster and because I was going to be in France already I said I'd ride her. In the end they decided not to run her so I thought, to hell with it, I'll take the day for myself. Although it's a very good card at Chantilly, I don't think I'll be missing out. On another day I might well have said something different. In fact, my ability to turn down races is about as effective as my ability to win a race without a horse.

Anyway, I'm really looking forward to it. I'm going to go showjumping in the morning in Addington in Buckinghamshire, then I'll come back in the afternoon and watch Wimbledon followed by the European Cup final. It's Spain versus England and who I'll be cheering for will depend solely on which squad has the most Chelsea players in it.

I've been getting a bit of feedback just recently about a docuseries I appeared in that's on Amazon Prime and now

BBC iPlayer called *Horsepower*. It's a similar format to the Formula 1 series *Drive to Survive*, which I'm a fan of, and follows the life and career of Andrew Balding and me (as well as one or two people who work for Andrew) from the autumn of 2020 until the summer of 2021. I'm not sure how popular it's been audience-wise, but the feedback I've been receiving has been unanimously positive.

I must admit, it was a little bit daunting when they started filming the series. I had cameras with me from the moment I got up in the morning until the moment I went to bed, seven days a week. In the end I just got used to it and was able to act as if they weren't there. The series itself lasts just four episodes at an hour apiece so they've only used a fraction of the footage. I watched a few bits of it and I must say I was very impressed. Not with me but with the production itself. It gives a very accurate insight into the relationship I have with Andrew Balding and a clear depiction of the stresses we were both under at the time.

It obviously wasn't planned but one of the main storylines in the series is a potential ban that's looming over me after having initially tested positive for cocaine in 2020. This was covered extensively in the press but a lot of that coverage was skewed and in some cases either untrue or just fabricated. Many of you reading this will probably remember the story but in the interests of fact I'd like to give my side.

In June 2020 I won the Qipco 2,000 Guineas on Kameko for Andrew and Qatar Racing. I'd already won twenty Group 1 races but winning a Classic for Andrew and Sheikh Fahad was something very special indeed. The adrenaline rush I experienced afterwards surpassed the one I had when Uncle Jim won the Grand National. It seemed to last for days and was undoubtedly enhanced by the effect the win had on Andrew and his staff. All of us were just over the moon. It was a tremendous time.

About six weeks later on 19 July, I was riding over in Chantilly and was required to provide a urine sample before the first race. Each racing authority will have its own rules as to how often this testing takes place, but in the UK it happens once a month, sometimes more frequently, and we're used to it.

I came away from Chantilly obviously thinking no more about the test. Then, on 19 August while I was up at York riding Kameko in the Juddmonte International Stakes, I received a WhatsApp message from my sister, Bláithín. A letter had arrived from France Galop and she'd opened it and sent me a photo. I can read French pretty well and it stated that the urine sample I'd provided at Chantilly had tested positive for metabolites of cocaine and could I contact them as soon as possible.

That evening after the races I called Andrew Balding, David Redvers who manages Qatar Racing and Sheikh Fahad to let them know what had happened and to assure them that I was innocent. I then contacted the PJA who advised me to have a hair sample taken for independent analysis. The resulting report would cover a three-month period and although it wouldn't override the results of the test taken in France, it would definitely be a sensible move. I agreed and organized it immediately. After all, had I taken cocaine would I really agree to something like this? Obviously not. It was the perfect way to proclaim my innocence.

As well as being conducted by an independent company and in front of two independent witnesses, the process was also recorded on video and then sent away for analysis. I also employed a French lawyer. Four days later I received the results of the test which proved conclusively that I had not taken cocaine in the last three months. Further correspondence with France Galop through the PJA revealed that they intended to test the B Sample (we always give two). Bearing in mind that this came from the same batch of urine as the A Sample, the result was a fait accompli. Sure enough, Sample B came back the same and I was charged by France Galop for testing positive for metabolites of cocaine.

At first I was shocked and alarmed by what had happened. I had never taken cocaine in my life and had been enjoying the best few months of my career. Why on earth would I, not even jeopardize but ruin my career by doing something so incredibly stupid? Testing takes place regularly so you'd almost certainly get caught, particularly in France. There's no hiding place these days.

But if I was innocent, you might be asking yourselves, how did cocaine get into my system?

The night before going to France I'd slept with a girl who had taken what must have been quite a large amount of cocaine and somewhere along the way a trace of that had been absorbed by me. Just to put it into perspective, the amount of cocaine we're talking about here, had I been tested in Britain, I wouldn't have failed the test. It was minuscule, but the testing threshold is lower in France and I just had to accept it. If I race in a different country it's up to me to familiarize myself with their rules, not the other way around, and if I fall foul of not doing so it's my own fault.

What I was actually guilty of in this matter was putting myself in an environment where cocaine was present and knowing that was the case I should have left the place immediately. I didn't though. Worse still, I ended up spending the night with somebody who'd been taking the stuff.

As you'd imagine, I would have preferred to keep something like this under wraps for a while. It wasn't to be, though, and on 1 October, the news broke to the press. This came as somewhat of a relief at first as it felt like I'd been carrying an enormous weight on my shoulders. That relief was short-lived and the reaction from the press, not to mention the public, was bigger and more immediate than I anticipated. As with the night in question, I'd judged this incorrectly.

It's astonishing how pious some people become when a story like this breaks. It presents an opportunity though, whereby a commentator or a member of the press (or public for that matter) can signal their own virtue via a controversial topic such as drugs in sport to the masses, hang the accused out to dry and at the same time help to sell a shedload of advertising and ingratiate themselves to their paymasters. Never mind about things such as facts or whether or not the person is guilty, or even if there were extenuating circumstances. These paragons of virtue who seem to delight in being outraged by the mere suggestion that somebody might have transgressed usually can't wait to pass sentence. Some of the commentary I heard after the story broke was incredible, but not in a good way.

My two heroes, Frankie Dettori and Kieren Fallon, had both served suspensions after testing positive for cocaine and according to the press I was the next one to fall from grace. Incidentally, the common denominator with both Frankie and Kieren is that they've both admitted to having taken the drug when they were at a very low ebb. I'm not excusing what they did, nor am I claiming that a jockey has never taken drugs for purely recreational purposes. Sometimes, though, you have to consider the reasons why an athlete might do such a thing and in terms of jockeys you'll often arrive at either depression or anxiety.

In 2021 the *British Medical Journal* conducted a study into the mental health difficulties of professional jockeys. The results of the study indicated that jockeys reported 'higher levels of depressive and anxiety symptoms compared with other elite athletes'. Substance misuse and in particular excessive alcohol use also appeared greater among jockeys than among other elite athletes. It went on to say that risk factors for mental health difficulties include 'injury, perceived stress, athlete burnout, career dissatisfaction and the contemplation of retirement', and that weight-making 'negatively impacts jockeys' mood and attitudes towards eating, with lower competitive riding weights associated with more disordered eating attitudes. Moreover, help-seeking from mental health professionals appears low.'

The report concluded that it had identified 'a high prevalence of symptoms of mental health difficulties among professional jockeys', which was no great surprise.

As soon as the story broke I was encouraged by the PJA to release a statement which I duly did. It read:

'I have never taken cocaine in my life and I will do everything that I can to prove that I have not taken cocaine. I want to thank those who are supporting me and in the meantime I want to keep riding winners and focus on my career. I will have no further comment to make and wish to respect the processes of France Galop.'

What affected me most just after it went public wasn't what

the press were saying, it was what the public were saying. People went online saying that I deserved to die and I even received the odd death threat. There were messages of support among it all but they were in the minority at first. It was vitriol on an industrial scale and I took it all to heart. How can you not when it seems like the majority of the people who follow the sport you love and have dedicated your life to are against you?

Despite the above, I was far more concerned about how the people closest to me might react, as well as my fellow professionals. In the end I needn't have worried. Everybody without exception – from Andrew and Anna Lisa, David and Sheikh Fahad to the staff at the yards and tracks and my colleagues in the weighing room – was universally supportive.

Four of the first people to call me after it went public were Frankie Dettori, Kieren Fallon, Rab Havlin and Kieran Shoemark, all of whom had been in a similar situation. They told me that it would all blow over and that I should keep my head down, fight my corner if I had to and come back stronger. At the time it felt like my career was in danger of imploding, so it was exactly what I needed to hear and from exactly the right people. It made a huge difference.

The biggest worry initially, about not only my future but also Andrew's, was that if France Galop did not accept the fact that I had been inadvertently contaminated by cocaine, then I was facing a six-month ban which would come into effect in mid-November and so preclude me from taking part in the start of the new season and crucially Guineas weekend. If that came to pass then the fallout would be massive. I remember sitting in Andrew and Anna Lisa's kitchen having a cup of tea and joking about what I might do during my suspension (Andrew suggested I take up painting), but the truth of the matter was that for the sake of his business, Andrew's loyalty to me would eventually be compromised if I couldn't fulfil my part of our partnership. Nobody ever said as much but it was definitely something I worried about.

One thing this episode did not affect was my performance as a jockey. It was the only thing I still had full control over at the time and if I was going to get banned for six months I was determined that it would happen while I was at the very top of my game. Another consideration was the championship which I led at the time but not by much. William and Tom were both nipping at my heels and I allowed myself to obsess about maintaining that lead in order to take my mind off the obvious.

In the end I managed to get over the line but there was no presentation of the trophy. I obviously presented a bad image for horse racing and as disappointing as that was, I actually understood and respected the decision. Regardless of the circumstances, you cannot hand over a trophy for the most successful athlete in a sport if said athlete is up on a drugs charge. That was the price for me having allowed myself to be in an environment where drugs were being taken and if I'd been in charge of the PJA I'd have done exactly the same thing.

The date for my hearing was eventually made for Wednesday 25 November. I went there expecting it to result in a six-month ban with the hope that it might be reduced to three. But I genuinely had no idea how it might go, nor did my lawyer. Not that they tell you immediately. The decision is usually made a few days later.

On Friday 27 November, I received the news that I had

been banned by France Galop for three months starting on 11 December. A statement from the authority said: 'France Galop stewards have banned Oisin Murphy from race-riding for three months after a biological sample taken on 19 July 2020 at Chantilly revealed the presence of cocaine metabolites. In accordance with the rules of racing of France Galop, the ban will take effect from 11 December 2020 until 11 March 2021 inclusive. This decision takes into account the defence and scientific evidence presented by the jockey and his counsel during a hearing on 25 November 2020, at the France Galop headquarters.'

Shortly after receiving the news I released my own state-ment via the PJA, which read: 'I would like to thank France Galop for accepting the evidence I presented that I had not taken cocaine. This evidence included my hair sample results, the results of which I am making public today, and an expert witness statement from an eminent toxicology and anti-doping expert. Whilst I am obviously disappointed that I will still have to serve a three-month suspension, I am pleased the Commissioners accepted the evidence presented and am hugely relieved to have been cleared of taking cocaine. I respect the rules of France Galop, respect their decision and will not be appealing. Despite my relief, I regretfully put myself in a situation whereby cocaine has been able to filter into my system through environmental contamination and must live with the consequences. As a professional sportsman I cannot put myself in a similar situ-ation again. Even though I have been exonerated from taking cocaine, I would like to take this opportunity to apologize to Sheikh Fahad al Thani, David Redvers and Andrew Balding and thank them for their support. Finally, I would also like to apologize to the whole Qatar Racing team, to the owners and trainers I ride for, my supporters, my weighing room colleagues and to my commercial partners as well as Racing to School. The next three months will give me much time to reflect on my actions but I will learn from this experience and come back better and even more determined than before.'

The fact that France Galop had accepted that I did not take cocaine came as much of a relief to me as the news that I had been suspended for three months instead of six. Regardless of what some members of the press and public were undoubtedly going to say about the decision (even to this day I'm referred to by many online trolls as a junkie or a druggie and it'll probably stick forever), to me it was vitally important. I'd done something stupid and had been punished for it. It was time to move on.

FIVE

Heroes

En route to Newmarket

RIDING FIVE DIFFERENT WINNERS FOR five different trainers at Newmarket was a huge thrill last week but
I was brought back down to earth very quickly by drawing
a blank at Ascot on Saturday and then at Longchamp. No
fewer than four of my rides that day were favourites so it
was pretty demoralizing. It doesn't matter how robust you
are mentally, that kind of thing is going to have an effect
on you. Tamfana at Longchamp was the biggest disappointment. She just didn't stay and I was sure she would. It just
goes like that sometimes. I thought I had the perfect trip
and if you'd asked me where I wanted to sit, how strong I
wanted the pace to be and what I wanted the ground to be
like I wouldn't have changed a thing. Unfortunately though
we just couldn't get it done.

Despite the above, this week has actually been really good
so far, both in terms of winners, sleep and my overall mood.

That's quite surprising really as last Saturday night and Sunday I was really down.

The only thing worrying me a bit today is that I'm racing at Newmarket and not Newbury. As well as being a lot closer to home I'd have had a lot of really good chances there. Also, the last race at Newmarket is at 8.40pm so I won't be home until late. What dictates where I ride is usually the quality of the racing, so if there's a Listed race or a Group race somewhere that's where I'll go.

As well as recording entries for this book, which I've been doing quite a lot lately, I usually kill time on these journeys by calling family and friends, reading the news or sending emails. I have a fairly short attention span though so I'll probably switch between the three dozens of times. There's always plenty to be getting on with so if I ever get bored it's because I've allowed myself to. I also have 8st 8lb today and am down for an 8st 6lb tomorrow so it's important that I keep myself distracted, not just from wasting but from the effect that the resulting dehydration has on me. I'd say a fairly large proportion of my bad moods are a result of that.

I've been asked on numerous occasions before why I don't just up my weight a bit and pick and choose what I ride. For a start there are horses in handicaps that carry light weights that I always like to ride and I'd also have to think seriously about going to America where the weights are generally lower: 8st 7lb and 8st 6lb are the norm over there and if you're not doing those kind of weights semi-regularly you're going to struggle. It's trying to find a lesser of two evils I suppose. You can either normalize the suffering by doing it all the time (while not ideal at least there are no nasty surprises) or you can ease that pain slightly for periods of time by paying the price of putting yourself through purgatory when you have to lose five or six pounds. It's each to their own of course but the former suits me better at the moment.

By far the biggest boost for me this week was a short interview that Kieren Fallon gave to the *Racing Post* in which he said that he expects me to prevail in the championship. Kieren's assessment of how nailed on my victory is differs from mine greatly, but the sentiment means a lot. I've already said that Kieren has been a hero of mine since I was a boy, but he was also my family's second favourite jockey to Uncle Jim and my grandfather on my mother's side idolized him. Learning that somebody of Kieren's stature rates you so highly is an enormous honour – the ultimate accolade really – and makes the work and sacrifice worthwhile.

The effect that Kieren's words had on me was that I went out and rode three winners so if he'd like to do it again, perhaps two or three times a week until at least the end of the season, I'd be very grateful.

The only other news this week is that my father is in hospital which is obviously a concern. He's had a heart condition for many years and has had several heart attacks. At first I felt a bit guilty about swanning around Europe while he's lying there in a hospital bed, but came to the conclusion quickly that I'm much more use to him riding horses and giving myself something to tell him when we speak than I would be sitting by his bed thinking of what to say. That's certainly what my father would want.

This did actually get me thinking about how incredibly intensive racing is these days. Tennis players get a day off, footballers get a day off, Formula 1 drivers get a day off, golfers get a day off. I'm not saying that these people don't work hard in between matches, races or tournaments, but horse racing is seven days a week and if you want to succeed at it you have to commit and follow suit. Even on the days of the year when there is no racing in the UK, you could probably ride in somewhere else like the Middle East. This isn't a complaint, by the way, just a recent observation.

I'm riding a horse called Sword tonight for the Gosdens which I stand half a chance on. There isn't a lot of pace in the race but if I can get him to relax and follow Jim Crowley and Jack Mitchell (if they race close together) and get off the back of the one that's going best, we could easily win. Another one of my rides tonight, Cuban Melody, won't like the track in my opinion, although she's the clear favourite. Then there's Capo Vaticano, who's one of Andrew's. She's a little bit light in the mouth but if she races the right way and relaxes she might go well, although again I'm not sure the track is ideal for her. If I didn't have to touch her mouth she'd be my best chance. Let's hope I can get one on the board. Anyway, we're almost at the track so I'd better get myself sorted.

FRIDAY, 26 JULY 2024

Lambourn, sweating in the bath

I've got 8st 11lb today, 8st 9lb tomorrow and then 8st 8lb on the first day at Goodwood next week, hence me having to sweat quite a bit. In contrast to the week before last I've been sleeping terribly last week and this. My mood has also been well below par and my energy levels have been appalling, particularly at Wolverhampton on Tuesday. The racing was messy and rough and despite my best efforts I struggled even to put a smile on my face. I felt guilty afterwards as there were a lot of people who were excited to be there. I just felt so down and so lethargic. No energy at all.

The only respite I've had in terms of sleep this week was a three-hour nap I had in between riding out on Wednesday and then travelling to Salisbury. That made a big difference to both my energy levels and my mood and got me through the day. Had it not happened I'd have gone to the meeting like I had Wolverhampton, just ten times worse. As it was, I came away with three winners and a spring in my step which was good.

Yesterday I benefitted from a bit of nepotism after being asked to ride a horse called Lil Guff in the first race at Sandown. The owner, Laura Clifford-Ward, is a close friend of my sister, Bláithín. Heaven only knows where they got the name of the horse from but we ended up winning the race comfortably. Thank you, Bláithín and Laura.

I've got Ascot today and tomorrow and both days will be very competitive. I've got bits of chances but it wouldn't surprise me if I drew a blank. That's not me being unduly pessimistic. Just realistic. Tactician in the second race today could easily win, so long as he tries. New Century, who is by Kameko and runs tomorrow, I like a lot, although I'm aware that over seven furlongs there might be some faster horses than him. I view New Century next year as being a mile or even a mile and a quarter horse. He's a half-sibling to Passion And Glory so he's bred to go a bit further, but his work has been very good. I just hope Andrew can keep on performing. I haven't got too stressed about Goodwood yet but at the same time it'll be important to get results there.

I don't know how many really well-handicapped horses we have at the moment, but let's see what happens.

With regards to the big race tomorrow, I've ridden in the King George VI and Queen Elizabeth Stakes many times before, but never on a horse that I thought I could win on. My ride, Middle Earth, really needs to step up after his performance at Royal Ascot. Even with a career best he's going to find the likes of Rebel's Romance and Auguste Rodin too good if they're flying. Middle Earth is a horse that I know can get to a high level and his job after Saturday is to go down under to Australia and possibly race in either the Melbourne Cup or the Caulfield Cup.

SUNDAY, 4 AUGUST 2024

En route to Deauville

Following on from my last entry, there was no joy at Ascot unfortunately. New Century did well by finishing second (I'm right, he's a mile or a mile and a quarter horse) but Middle Earth showed no improvement whatsoever since Royal Ascot. It'll be interesting to see how he gets on in Australia.

I faired a lot better at Goodwood I'm pleased to say. Goodwood is a very important meeting to me and I've enjoyed a fair amount of success there over the years. I've won the Sussex Stakes twice. Lightning Spear in 2018 for David Simcock and Alcohol Free for Andrew in 2021. I also won the Nassau Stakes on a Japanese horse called Deirdre in 2019. The weather's almost always excellent at Goodwood (or at least at this meeting) which affects the atmosphere.

My favourite memory from Goodwood as a spectator is the legendary 'Duel on the Downs'. The year was 2011 and Frankel and Canford Cliffs were going head to head in the Sussex Stakes. At the time I was over in Ireland so was still dreaming about riding in such big races. Canford Cliffs hung like a gate off his line which was unfortunate but the build-up to the race was amazing.

This year I came away with four wins, which I was happy with, and one three-day suspension, which I wasn't. The suspension came after the Coral Golden Mile which I actually won on a David Menuisier horse called Toimy Son. When Toimy Son was drawn twenty-one out of twenty-one, David was despondent. I had it in my head though that if I could just get inside his brain on the way to post and really wake him up we might stand a chance. I took my time on him and when I switched out into space he really took off. He hadn't been trying too hard in his previous races so was well handicapped and I managed to make the difference on him.

The interference which led to the suspension was annoying to say the least. Toimy Son's a very small horse and when he moved unexpectedly I didn't have much of a saddle on him. He didn't actually make contact with another horse but he caused Holloway Boy to come off his line and as a result I got the blame. I corrected him as early as I could and on any other day I might have got away with it. On this occasion I didn't though. It's just one of those things.

I'm on my way to Deauville at the moment where I have three rides today. They are all fillies looking for black type (Group, Graded or Listed races) and are all outside chances so there's no great expectation. I'm sharing a small plane with Richard Hughes who trains about 200 metres from my home in Lambourn. We often travel to the races together. If he's booking a small plane or a helicopter I'll hitch a ride, even if I'm not riding for him.

I had an inordinate amount of admiration for Richard as a jockey. He was always in control and had a supreme air of confidence that I believe was integral to the success he had with Richard Hannon. He had the lot though. Finesse, tactical brilliance, style. He went through the card at Windsor, won races all over the world and had the Juddmonte job. He also managed his weight like no one I've ever known before. Just to rub salt into the wound from my own point of view as a sportsman, he also plays off scratch at golf, or at least he used to. It wouldn't surprise me in the slightest if he still does.

It's only since I met my difficulties with alcohol that I started to get to know Richard. During my ban he'd text me while I'd still be in bed at half past six in the morning and ask me if I'd like to pop out and ride one, which I always did. Like me, Richard is a recovering alcoholic and has been sober for a very long time. He, more than anyone else I know, understands what drove me to such a dark place and his support during my ongoing recovery has been invaluable. Nothing has ever been too much trouble and as well as trusting him implicitly my respect for Richard, both as a jockey and a trainer but especially as a human being, is immeasurable. He's an inspiration.

If Richard ever has a horse that he wants an opinion on he'll ask me. As well as being a bit of an honour, it affords me the opportunity to repay just a little bit of the kindness he's shown me over the years. What he's done for the apprentices he's turned professional such as Finley Marsh and George

Rooke is also extraordinary. With some trainers the support might waver until you prove yourself, but he's been fully behind those lads. I also think he's a very good trainer. Last year was his best ever season, not only numerically but also statistically and he also won more black type races than ever before. Anyway, The Richard Hughes Fan Club will no doubt reconvene here in Volume II.

I've been asked on quite a few occasions over the years if I would ever take up training myself and the answer would have to be yes. I *would* take up training, but only if the circumstances were absolutely spot on. As you know, my earliest influence in horse racing was my Uncle Jim and I've learned just as much from him about training as I have being a jockey. One of the first lessons I learned was how much pressure trainers have to endure. It truly is relentless.

As a jockey I have to watch my weight, communicate effectively with various people, get to and from meetings on time and perform to the best of my ability. It can be tough going sometimes but at the end of the day the only person I'm responsible for is me. Trainers are on the other end of the scale really. In addition to being responsible for all the staff they employ they also have to negotiate with jockeys (not an easy task at the best of times), owners, suppliers, the BHA, vets and God knows who else. They're also responsible for the horses, the infrastructure, the equipment and the machinery. Have I missed something? Probably lots of things. Add to that the fact that their very existence is fully dependent on them maintaining a certain level of success and you have on your hands a recipe for pressure on an industrial scale.

Having observed the likes of Andrew, Aidan O'Brien,

Harry Charlton, John Gosden, David Menuisier and others over a number of years, I know how hard it can be. One of the reasons they're successful though is because they're able to soak up that pressure and allow the aforementioned people to get on with their jobs. It's an all-consuming occupation to which you willingly give all of your time and energy.

Attracting and then retaining owners is one of the hardest tasks on a trainer's plate. It's a partnership that is reliant on building confidence and if that confidence doesn't material-ize somewhere along the way the chances are the owner will go elsewhere. In that respect it's like being a jockey because if you don't deliver the goods somebody else will take your place, and there's plenty out there of both.

I've seen owner/trainer relationships where that con-fidence is in abundance and it's a joy to behold. After all, success tends to breed success so as well as that particular relationship thriving it can generate new ones. That's obvi-ously how trainers become successful and is what has taken Andrew from being a fairly successful trainer with ninety horses to one of the most successful trainers in the country with about 250 horses. There's no let-up though. Maintain-ing and building on his success (or at least some aspect of it) will be the last thing he thinks of when he goes to bed and the first thing he thinks of when he wakes up. I guarantee it.

Conversely, I have also been witness to relationships between trainers and owners where that confidence is sadly lacking. Sometimes it's down to a lack of success, but it can also be down to a clash of personalities or a failure to manage expectations. It must be very tempting to tell a prospective owner what they want to hear in order to seal a deal. It'll come back to bite you, though.

One of my earliest ambitions was to own my own stables by the age of twenty-five and I managed to do that when I bought Frenchman's House and Stables in Lambourn. Knowing what I know now, if I were to take up training I'd have to dip my toe in the water and start in a very small way. My fear of failure wouldn't allow me to do it any other way I'm afraid. I have good connections and a fairly wide knowledge of the industry and of horses but that wouldn't necessarily translate to me being a successful trainer. Far more intelligent people than me have failed at training horses and I'm well aware of that.

I find the difference that exists between trainers very interesting. Some are very hard on horses (as in workload) and some are very easy. Some rarely move off the routine whereas others are happy to do different things with horses every day. John Gosden and Aidan O'Brien are both routine trainers. They tend to use the same gallops and will walk, trot and warm down for a long time whereas other trainers have quicker lots and are equally successful. Richard Fahey is a serious trainer and so is Kevin Ryan, and their lots would be much shorter than Gosden's or O'Brien's. They charge less as a daily rate and have fewer staff so they've more to get through. Andrew and Ralph Beckett also have shorter lots and they're also system trainers. Andrew gallops his horses routinely (the older horses maybe twice a week) whereas Ralph sometimes just canters his horses and week to week he might not gallop that many. No two trainers are the exact same and all will have different approaches and different methods.

Harry Charlton is very methodical in his approach. He's a thinker. Archie Watson's a very good race planner which means he does well with low-level horses (as well as high-level horses). David Menuisier is very good with horses later in the year as his strike rate in the autumn is just phenomenal. He doesn't do anything differently early doors so I have no idea why it happens like that.

If I were thinking seriously about becoming a trainer I'd probably study the ones I've just mentioned very carefully indeed, think about it long and hard and then decide to avoid it like the plague and carry on being a jockey! It's a similar situation to buying and selling horses really. On paper it might seem like a great opportunity but there's a devil or two waiting within the detail. Approach with caution.

I have 8st 8lb today and I've had 8st 9lb or less every day since Tuesday. I'm mindful not to go on about the weight and wasting issue too much but the simple fact is that it's as omnipresent in my life as my desire to finish first. Hollie Doyle is a brilliant and talented jockey and a gorgeous human being, but every time I look at her I can't help thinking to myself, you lucky devil! She's only five foot tall so her natural weight is obviously a lot closer to her riding weight. I'm not saying she has it easy though. Far from it. Whereas the likes of me have to address the disparity between our natural weight and riding weight by wasting, because of her stature Hollie has to work incredibly hard to keep her strength. I was reading a profile on her just the other day and as well as being able to jump her own height, which is impressive, apparently she can deadlift over twice her own weight. That's sixteen stone plus. Incredible.

I slept very well last night but I'm absolutely exhausted. A combination of a run of seconds, which exhausts me mentally, making light weights and the workload have taken their toll. Yesterday was very similar but it was rewarding to finish Goodwood as leading rider. This week is ordinary stuff. I'll be galloping Kikkuli for Harry Charlton on Thursday morning at Kempton with the hope of partnering him on Saturday week in the Hungerford Stakes at Newbury. I just hope I can get my strike rate up a bit this coming week on those ordinary days. Being a realist though, it could be a slow week. There's not a lot jumping out at me.

With regards to the championship, it's firmly in my mind. It's the first thing I think about as I wake up and the last thing as I go to bed. I genuinely don't believe my lead will be enough and I need to keep the momentum going. Rossa Ryan and in particular Tom Marquand will have a good August. William too will have plenty of favourites to ride in novices and maidens. I wonder if it plays on their minds as much as it does mine. I'm sure it does.

TUESDAY, 6 AUGUST 2024

En route to Chelmsford

I've just been watching the final of the men's Olympic individual showjumping in Paris and it's been carnage. Mexico's Andres Azcarraga only narrowly avoided being thrown into the water, whereas the best rider in the world, Sweden's Henrik von Eckermann, was sent flying into an obstacle.

As they shaped to jump, Azcarraga's horse turned to the side and sent him flying. He managed to hold on to the reins so only his feet swung into the water. It was a narrow escape though. The commentator put it down to the horse being spooked by the water glinting. Usually when you're approaching water, the filler on the front of the jump is either solid or open, whereas this one had a gap and so all the horse must have seen was the light shining through it.

As dramatic as that was, the incident involving Henrik von Eckermann was a far bigger surprise. He's been the world number one for the last two years and his horse, King Edward, is probably the best there is. Henrik appeared to change his mind halfway down a line of jumps. The horse then got a fright, they lost connection and they departed from each other. The commentator said that they hadn't looked confident yesterday but didn't suggest a reason. Pressure of the Olympics, I should think. I don't envy him. Actually, of course I do. I'd love to compete in showjumping at the Olympics. It'll never happen though. The truth is I have a lot more confidence than skill when showjumping. I'll give you an example.

In 2022 while I was suspended, I rode a horse called Medusa in the Hickstead Speed Derby. It was in the main arena so there were over five thousand spectators and I was confident she'd win the class. Everything went well until fence number six which comprised two vertical fences on a bit of a bank. On the last stride she put the brakes on and I fell off over her head and took the bridle with me. While I sat there mortified, Medusa galloped around the main arena loose. I was so disgusted with myself that I didn't even try and catch her. Michael Duffy did in the end. I just walked slowly out of the ring with my head down and barely spoke for the rest of the day. Not one of my better days.

I've just set off to Chelmsford for two races on their all-weather course. Traffic permitting it'll probably take about three hours to get there, although it could take longer to get back. I'll be leaving the track just before 7pm so heaven knows what state the M25 will be in. The quality of the horses I'm riding this evening isn't good either (I've got one for Andrew and one for Hughie Morrison) but what can you do? Seven or eight hours for not very much reward, either financial or professional.

You might be asking why I give myself such a punishing workload. Is it simply because of the championship, or is it more to do with a love of horse racing? First of all, nobody falls in love with travelling six hours to and from Chelmsford on a Tuesday. Not unless you like boredom and traffic. Part of my motivation for doing what I do is because I love racing. The other part, as I think I've already stated more than once, is my competitive nature. What fuels that (the motivation behind the motivation, you might say) has changed over the years and each time I've gone for champion jockey there's been something different driving me. When I first set out I had a point to prove, not just to me but to the whole world. I wanted to assail the gates of horse racing, jump over the drawbridge, kill the enemy (metaphorically) and swing from the chandeliers. After all, it's every jockey's dream to win the championship and if you think you even have the slightest chance, you go for it. That was my motivation when I won it for the first time in 2019. Letting the world know that I was on the scene and could mix it with the best.

What fuelled my second and third wins in 2020 and 2021 was even more potent, if that were possible. You know what it's like, when you have something nice you want to keep hold of it. That was me and the championship, basically. I adored being the best in the UK (numerically) and I wanted to remain where I was. The strength of my desire to achieve this was down to the fact that once you're at the top of your game, there's only one way to go and that's down. I was desperate to win again but I was also desperate not to lose. This made the victory even sweeter.

When I tried to regain the championship in 2023 it was back to having to prove myself again. When I got suspended I had to watch everyone else riding winners for fourteen months which was torturous and I was still slated online pretty much constantly. When I came back I wanted to prove to those people, and to myself, that I was as hungry as ever and was still a force to be reckoned with. It didn't quite work out in the end as William remained in imperious form all season and beat me by twenty-nine wins.

My motivation this year is more nuanced. Despite finishing second in 2023, my performance in general wasn't up to standard (my strike rate was just 17 per cent compared to William's strike rate of 22 per cent) and as well as wanting to prove to myself and everyone else that I can ride as well as I did in 2019, 2020 and 2021, I just want to be better. It's a self-respect thing, I suppose. Sure, I love being called Champ by my fellow jockeys. Who wouldn't love that? Being able to look myself in the mirror though and be satisfied that I've done everything in my power to give myself the best possible chance of succeeding is equally important. That's what got me in the car this afternoon to travel to Chelmsford and is what got me to Lingfield yesterday. A desire to win but also a desire to do myself justice. I could easily have made an excuse or taken a sickie but as long as there's even a slim chance of me getting a win, I'll go where I have to.

It's probably one of the reasons why I feel relief more than euphoria when I win, especially these days. I once read an interview with a racing driver who won the Le Mans 24 Hour. He put so much effort into winning the race that he collapsed at the end through exhaustion and so didn't manage to attend the presentation ceremony. That'll probably be me if I win the championship this year. My memory of the presentation ceremonies in 2020 and 2021 has always been pretty scant so I've been building up to it.

The question I'm asking myself at the moment is, *How am I going to feel if I do win it for a fourth time?* The initial emotion will be relief as always (with a hint of euphoria, I hope) but then, what next? Will I be able to take my foot off the gas and be happy with four? Or, for the sake of professional pride, will I want to keep going? As I said earlier, once you're at the top there's only one place you can go and nobody wants to go that way. Then again, nothing in this world lasts forever. I appreciate that. If I do decide to ease up a bit then I'll have to make sure there's something in place that will satisfy my competitive nature and push me to the limit professionally, and hopefully without killing me.

MONDAY, 12 AUGUST 2024

Lambourn

This last week or so has been awful mood-wise. I've been so up and down. I was in two minds this morning whether to talk about this as I know I'll be repeating myself but I have to be honest about the turmoil of a life in racing. At least for me. It tends to be driven by energy, as in how much I have or haven't got. Take yesterday, for instance. After a good night's sleep I woke up at the crack of dawn full of enthusiasm. I went to nine o'clock Mass, collected a friend from Ascot and dropped him off at his house, then had my sister over for lunch. After she left, the high started to wear off. I did my best to remain sociable and upbeat but by the evening I was as flat as a pancake and I've woken up this morning feeling exactly the same. Funnily enough, this was how I felt last Monday and Tuesday so perhaps it's a beginning of the week thing. Or perhaps not. If only it were that simple.

So many of the things in my life have to be forced. Nothing's natural. If my mood is poor, which it often is at the races or when I'm flat, I'll force myself to smile. I'll then force myself not to eat or drink for heaven knows how long before forcing myself to sit in the bath for two hours and then force myself to sit in a car for six more. Once I've finished this entry I'll have to force myself to answer the twenty-four individual WhatsApp messages that were waiting for me when I switched my phone on a couple of hours ago, and communicate with my manager, Jimmy Derham, about emails and admin. Sometimes I yearn to just be myself without fear of upsetting somebody, letting people down or getting into trouble.

The common denominator with all this is that this tends to happen after a good spell and this is no exception. Last Thursday I galloped a Kingman horse by Passage Of Time for Harry Charlton at Kempton which put me on an incredible high. What a horse! Later that day I had two good winners at Chepstow followed by another three at Haydock on Friday. Then, on Saturday, I won four of the six races on the card at Newmarket. Heck, I was flying. I can't remember when I had such an enjoyable few days. Not just in terms of winning, but in terms of fulfilment. I was so happy.

For the first time in my career I'm seriously considering stepping off the conveyor belt. Actually, that's a lie. I did think about it momentarily after the two big suspensions but that was more of a reaction to what had happened than a considered decision. This is actually the first time I've questioned why I'm doing what I do, to the point of me asking myself whether something else might exist that could keep me happy and fulfilled without the sacrifice and emotional investment.

As you know, until now I've always been driven by a yearning for success followed by more success. The cost of this, however, has been increasing of late, both emotionally and physically. The highs are still as great as ever but the lows are becoming unbearable. It's like hangovers when you get older, so I've been told. They get worse and worse and worse.

Because my mood changes so often and so dramatically I'll probably think differently in a couple of hours. In fact, I know I will. I'm already booking rides for the end of the year in places like India and Bahrain and it won't be long before I start looking at 2025. You see, I'm already trying to talk myself out of it. Then again, none of it is written in stone. The fact that I'm having this train of thought and am questioning what I do is something positive. In fact, if somebody had suggested to me a few months ago that it might be time for a change I'd have laughed at them. Anyway, let's see what occurs.

For all our sakes I'm going to finish this entry off with a positive statement that not even I can put a negative spin on. My strike rate is back up to 22 per cent which is exactly where I want it to be and I'm thirty-five wins ahead in the championship. Let's just leave it at that.

WEDNESDAY, 14 AUGUST 2024

Lambourn

I had no intention of recording an entry so soon after the last one but the last three days have been a nightmare and I need to get it off my chest. This time though it's had nothing to do with my fluctuating mood and everything to do with the fallout after being forced to miss two rides at Kempton on Monday due to illness and subsequently missing a breath test.

Way back at the start of July I started suffering from haemorrhoids. It's not something you expect to happen in your twenties and certainly not something you'd choose to go public with. Could you imagine the post on Instagram? 'Two good wins for Andrew today, spoilt slightly by the news that I'm suffering with piles. Thank God we don't have to sit down while we race!' I have no idea whether it's common among jockeys, although if it is, it wouldn't surprise me. Our unconventional diet and eating habits, not to mention the fact that we spend much of our life riding horses, would suggest it might be.

Apart from the odd uncomfortable day they hadn't been much of a problem, although I had had to wear a nappy from time to time. Then, on Sunday, they began to get quite painful and on Monday morning I woke up to find that I'd passed blood on to my sheets during the night. I'd passed blood regularly when going to the toilet since having haemorrhoids so it didn't worry me, but shortly after leaving the house for Kempton I noticed that my boxers were wet. I certainly hadn't peed myself. It was yet more blood.

I immediately called Andrew and my agent, Gavin, to let them know what was happening. This had happened once before and when it did I was taken to Chelsea and Westminster Hospital to see a specialist. 'I'm going to try and see the same man again,' I said to them, and then started making some calls.

While that was going on, Gavin made alternative arrangements for my rides and called the steward of the course to inform him of my absence. The steward then called me to find out how I was and what had been occurring and he was sound enough. The only potential issue was that I'd been due to take a breath test that day which would have to be postponed.

Because of my past I am tested more regularly than other jockeys. It's never been a problem for me, although the fact that I'm tested for drugs so often by the BHA is a little bit rich seeing as though the test that got me into trouble would have been negative had it taken place in the UK instead of France. Alcohol was my problem, not drugs. They seem obsessed by it and the additional testing will probably carry on for the rest of my career. It's bizarre really.

After the steward at Kempton had spoken to me and the other interested parties a report was written.

An inquiry was held to consider why Oisin Murphy, who was required to provide a breath sample, had failed to arrive. The sampling officer, the clerk of the scales and Murphy were interviewed, and the matter was forwarded to the Head Office of the British Horseracing Authority for further consideration.

As quick as a flash the report was picked up by the press (legitimately so) who obviously had a field day. Every single racing website and social media platform was full of the fact that Oisin Murphy had missed a breath test at Kempton and the ensuing outpouring of bile and speculative bullshit was as hurtful and annoying as it was predictable. 'It was only a matter of time.' 'Always knew he'd fall off the wagon.' 'Bet he's been on the piss for months.' 'Once an alky, always an alky.' You know the kind of thing. It was everywhere.

It was a proverbial guilty till proven innocent situation and after a few short hours it seemed to be a cut-and-dried case as far as certain members of the press and public were concerned. Oisin Murphy was back on the bottle and it was only a matter of time before an announcement was made. They must have been so disappointed it didn't materialize. In fact, a lot of them probably were.

While all this was going on, I took it upon myself to send photographic evidence of what had happened to the doctor at the BHA, Jerry Hill, together with proof that I had attended Chelsea and Westminster Hospital that morning. I didn't have to do this but in the interests of saving everybody time and trouble and making sure the BHA knew that I hadn't been pulling a fast one, I thought it was a good idea.

After submitting the photographs of my bloodied boxer shorts and proof that I had attended the hospital, instead of accepting my evidence and drawing a line under it immediately like I'd been expecting, the BHA obviously weren't convinced. An investigation was opened and on not one but two occasions that day the investigating officer called me up and asked me to go through the events again and re-substantiate my claim. The only reason I can think of as to why they would go to such lengths is because they were trying to catch me out. I mean, why else would they ask me to go over everything twice after having submitted photographic evidence of my complaint and proof that I'd attended hospital?

Their excuse would probably be that I'd lied to them in the past about going on holiday during Covid, which to be fair would probably carry some weight. After all, I did lie to them during Covid and I was punished accordingly. What annoys and upsets me though is that no other jockey in the country would be treated like this. This isn't sour grapes. I genuinely believe that and I'm certainly not the only one who does.

Funnily enough, taking a photograph of my boxer shorts with haemorrhoid blood on them and sending it to the doctor at the BHA hadn't been on my to-do list on Monday morning. Stupidly though, I believed that in addition to it being the right and proper thing to do, the BHA would say OK and perhaps even give me some credit for having done so. I certainly didn't think that they would question the validity of my reason and evidence and come back at me twice. It makes you think, *Why the hell do I bother?*

Because of what was happening with the press and on social media at 7pm on Monday, I was reluctantly forced to go public via social media with the news that I had been suffering with haemorrhoids. 'I've noticed blood in my breeches at the races recently,' I said, 'and have needed to change numerous times. This morning I noticed more blood than I'd seen before. I've got haemorrhoids. I'm fine and I'll be back riding tomorrow.'

The opinion among the press and members of the public that I'd started drinking again seemed so conclusive and this felt like my only course of action. In hindsight, I should probably have taken some advice first but I didn't. It was obviously very humiliating but I felt I had no choice.

Yesterday the headline in the *Racing Post* was typically supportive. 'Oisin Murphy reported to BHA head office after failing to arrive at Kempton when due to provide breath sample'. The *Mirror* and the *Telegraph* were slightly less sensationalist and both went with, 'Former champion jockey Oisin Murphy blames haemorrhoids for missing breathalyser test'.

An unusual bright spot in all of this has been the reaction to the message I posted on social media on Monday revealing what had happened. There were one or two insulting ones, obviously, but the vast majority of replies were supportive and some were even quite humorous. I was riding at Lingfield yesterday and one of the replies read: ANUSOL 2.30 LINGFIELD. Bottom Weight.

Look, I get why people might get a bit suspicious when a well-known jockey and recovering alcoholic who has served a lengthy ban fails to turn up for a breath test. But the way in which it spiralled out of control and was then covered was alarming to say the least. Had the BHA been more supportive and ready to accept my reasons without interrogating me twice, then it wouldn't have been quite so bad, but they didn't. In fact, the effect of their actions has had a more detrimental effect on me than the press and public. I dare say they'll get over it though.

I had three at Lingfield yesterday afternoon and as you'd expect all eyes were on me. I came away with nothing unfortunately, but the support I got in the weighing room was worth ten winners. It was exactly what I needed and helped to restore at least some of my faith in the sport.

TUESDAY, 20 AUGUST 2024

En route to Newmarket

I'm pleased to report that haemorrhoid-gate appears to have died a death and I've had no contact from the BHA on the matter since late last week. It's a pity that can't be said for the haemorrhoids themselves, although things are definitely getting better. A friend of mine asked me if the BHA had been in touch with me to see how I was feeling and I almost died laughing.

I went to Chelsea to watch the Manchester City game on Sunday. The result was disappointing (Chelsea lost 0–2) but it was nice to watch a different sport for a change. Particularly one that doesn't involve horses. Speaking of which. I went to the showjumping on Friday. A horse I own called Messento was clear with time faults and was very impressive. He was clear again yesterday and then won the jump-off for the half a million pound Grand Prix which impressed me even more.

I'm on my way to Newmarket at the moment to gallop Asfoora. I'm riding her in the Nunthorpe Stakes at York on Saturday and at the moment she's the 11/8 favourite. I hope they're right. It's being billed as a battle between Asfoora and Big Evs, but I don't think it'll be that simple. They're due a bit of rain at York over the next few days and Asfoora needs fast ground. She's a big heavy filly, but even if you see her cantering she skips across the floor and barely makes a mark on the surface. Despite her weight and size she's like a ballerina.

I've got plenty of rides at York but as always it's going to be really competitive. I always try not to set myself a target in terms of numbers at meetings like this, but I'd like to come away with a few. I'll not be greedy though. Queen Of The Pride is second favourite in the Yorkshire Oaks. Her work last time I rode her was unimpressive if I'm honest with you, but I'm hoping that's just her going through the motions. She's had a nice gap between her last win at Haydock and this race. There will be plenty of horses in the handicaps too, although it's a hard place to win.

I've already talked about how much I love York as a city, but it's also my favourite track, with Doncaster coming a very close second. I love the make-up of York. It's left-handed, very flat and the best horse usually wins. It also has a tremendous atmosphere and we jockeys are always very well looked after. The Clerk of the course, William Derby, is also fantastic and I've had some very happy times there.

People often assume that my least favourite track will be Newcastle or Wolverhampton. The inference being, I think, that because they're all-weather tracks we might be there on a wet Tuesday evening in February with just driving rain, a bitter north-easterly wind and a handful of spectators and bookies for company. I admit there have been times at those tracks, and others, when I've thought to myself, *What on earth am I doing here?* There's the same risk of injury and no reward, other than being able to lift the championship trophy on the third Saturday in October. Generally, you don't see the top jockeys at these meetings, unless they're there for a novice or a maiden and are hoping to find the next star.

Apart from just wanting to ride winners I appreciate the fact that a lot of the owners who are involved in the sport will own these lower-grade horses and it'll mean as much to them to win a normal race at Wolverhampton on a wet Tuesday evening in winter as it would the owner of a winner at Royal Ascot. Regardless of how I'm feeling internally I'll always try and rev myself up and be positive and make sure they all have a good experience, even if the horse runs badly. It'd be very easy to just wander out late into the paddock, say hi and get on the horse, then get off the horse at the end and run into the weighing room. In reality I've probably done that at stages through my career, but since coming back from the fourteen-month ban I've tried to ensure that every owner and trainer feels like I want to ride their horse. It's no more than what they all deserve.

By the way, my least favourite track would have to be Pontefract, but only because I feel I don't ride very well there.

With regards to my admiration of York, the Ebor Festival is the icing on the cake for me. I'll be staying with my friend Richard Howley who lives opposite Wetherby Racecourse. As well as being one of the best riders that Ireland has ever produced, Richard also looks after my showjumpers so as well as talking a lot about showjumping, I might get to do a bit too. I'm always more upbeat when I stay at Richard's. The last time I stayed there I went to Newcastle and had a treble. They're lovely people and it's a reminder that although my life is ruled by horses, it isn't just horse racing.

Although the Ebor meeting will be very full on, I'll be straight to Goodwood on Sunday. That meeting is normally very good to me and the prize money's pretty good too. It isn't comparable with York, of course, but it's always quite competitive and well worth the trip. Toimy Son, the fella I won the Coral Golden Mile Handicap on at Glorious

Goodwood is going to run again in another mile handicap and stands a really good chance.

The Juddmonte International Stakes, which normally takes place on the first day of the Ebor meeting, was once again voted the world's highest rated race, so the world's best race in other words. This is worked out by the average rating of the runners and is obviously a huge accolade for York.

The Juddmonte is the last middle-distance Qipco British Champions Series race before the Qipco Champion Stakes and I won it myself in 2018 on the amazing Roaring Lion. That was one of my best seasons to date in terms of Group 1 races as I won nine in five different countries.

Roaring Lion's run of form began in the Dante and in that race he was like a rocket. We were beaten in the Craven and the Guineas, but all of a sudden it started to click and I remember in the Dante he was really strong through the line. He didn't stay in the Derby, as feared. The pressure was on in the Eclipse but he prevailed and in the Juddmonte he was out of this world. The quality of horses he beat that day was just ridiculous. Poet's Word, Thundering Blue, Saxon Warrior, Thunder Snow and my old friend, Benbatl. He just travelled round at the back and then ran away from them late on. The ground too was perfect. Fast ground, flat track. I remember travelling to the track in a helicopter with Sheikh Fahad on the day. I'd barely slept a wink during the previous few nights because of the pressure I'd been under and I conked out on the way up there. At the end of the 2018 season, Roaring Lion was rated the best three-year-old in the world and the fourth best horse of any age or sex.

His next race after the Juddmonte was the Irish Champion Stakes which to this day is one of the most high-pressure situations I've ever been in. Four of the seven runners were trained by Aidan O'Brien, including Saxon Warrior. Roaring Lion and I were on a hat-trick and Aidan's army were out to spoil the party. We were sent off the 8/11 favourite, so they were going to have a job on their hands. I knew having done my homework that the race was going to be tactical. I was on the best horse though, I was sure of that. I just needed a clear run. In the end I had to challenge wide and the first run on us came from Saxon Warrior. Roaring Lion showed a massive turn of foot and from the bottom of the straight I knew we had it in the bag. The thing that was most extraordinary about Roaring Lion, apart from his ability in a race, was his temperament at the start. He never got wound up or became fractious. He would just walk round calmly with an air of supreme confidence. He was great in that respect. A pleasure to partner.

Roaring Lion and I made it four Group 1s in a row just over a month later and on the biggest stage of all by winning the Queen Elizabeth II Stakes at Ascot on Qipco British Champions Day. This is probably my favourite memory with Roaring Lion. It was a perfect day. When the stalls opened I was drawn out on the wing on my own. I had a high draw and the pace was all low and we quickly settled into the back of the midfield. Frankie made the running on Hey Gaman with Laurens and P J McDonald on board running second and Century Dream with William just covered up behind.

The first two furlongs went quite smoothly. Roaring Lion felt relaxed and I was happy with our position. That wouldn't last long though as the pace still wasn't strong and it's hard to make gains on very slow ground. The horse directly in front of us was Jim Crowley's mount Beat The Bank whom I knew well. He stood a good chance and so I decided to just keep behind him, bide my time and then creep into the race.

At the halfway stage, things were going very well. We hadn't over-raced but Frankie was beginning to stretch and things were starting to unfold. I gave Roaring Lion a squeeze but didn't want to get there too soon. I wanted to just coax him into the race.

As the new course reached the round course I was still on the bridle. Addeybb with James Doyle on board was on my inside and Recoletos with Olivier Peslier on my outside. At this point I just gave Roaring Lion a little tap on the shoulder with the stick. Olivier Peslier was now getting to work but Century Dream with William on board was the horse I set my sights on.

As we approached the final furlong, I pulled my stick through to my right hand and then straightened him up and got him balanced. At this point there were three of us still in it, but as soon as I asked him to go, he flew and at that point I knew we were going to win. It was such a good feeling to get the job done.

The icing on the cake that day, and with regards to my partnership with Roaring Lion, was having the trophy presented to me afterwards by Her Majesty Queen Elizabeth II. I'd already had the pleasure of meeting Her Majesty several times at Andrew's stables and at Ascot and she was very knowledgeable. She also cared deeply about horse racing and did the sport an incredible amount of good.

Winning the QEII Stakes was a fitting end to Roaring Lion's career on this side of the Atlantic, but as an American-bred horse it was decided that his swansong should be on home soil in the Breeders' Cup Classic. That race took place exactly a month after the QEII Stakes. He travelled well and trained well in the mornings, but the dirt came as a bit of a shock to him because apart from Kempton Park's all-weather track, he'd raced exclusively on turf. Moreover, that was his ninth start since April. He was tired out.

Roaring Lion went to stud after the Breeders' Cup with eight wins from twelve races to his name and career earnings totalling over £2.7 million. In 2019 he was sent out to New Zealand for the southern hemisphere breeding season, but shortly after leaving quarantine he became ill with colic (for which he'd had numerous operations) and had to be euthanized. The vets and the staff there did everything possible. It was a terrible shame but what a legacy. And what a horse!

I've just remembered that despite me waxing poetic about the Juddmonte, I don't actually have a ride in it this year. It's been nice to reminisce though.

SIX

You Win Some, You Lose Some

Wetherby

TWO WINS FROM THE FIRST three days is obviously a lot less than I was hoping for. Then again, apart from Ryan Moore absolutely killing it, no one else has been so it doesn't seem so bad. To be honest with you, I haven't even been unlucky on anything I've ridden. They just haven't been good enough. That makes it easier to accept in a way but it's still very frustrating.

It won't come as a surprise to learn that apart from Frankie I'm asked more questions about Ryan Moore than any other jockey. Not because he's a friend of mine, which he is, but because he's the best jockey in the world at the moment and has been for some time.

Ryan's very measured and has great self-control which prevents him from getting carried away by the ups and downs of racing. As one of the most successful jockeys of all time and the most successful in any current weighing room, there's a huge amount of pressure on him and he deals with it so well. He's also a family man and will sometimes bring his children to the races, particularly his son, Toby. Toby's also quite small and I'm sure will be a chip off the old block.

Ryan's had some of the biggest jobs in racing, working for the likes of Richard Hannon and Sir Michael Stoute to Aidan O'Brien. He's loyal, he rarely makes mistakes and pushes himself to make light weights. He's also incredibly strong, very intelligent and is probably the most tactically astute jockey in the world. He's got everything really.

From a personal point of view, I've always got on well with Ryan but even more so in recent years. During my fourteen-month suspension he sent me the odd text message to see how I was faring, and when I was due to race over jumps for the first time he wished me the best of luck.

He's often accused of being quiet and even miserable which is absolute rubbish. He's simply careful about what he says and to whom and doesn't suffer fools or care for stupid questions. We should all be more like him in that respect.

During races we have an understanding not to get in each other's way. For instance, if my horse is beginning to weaken I'll always try and give him some space and vice versa. Also, without ever discussing tactics or what each other is going to do before big races, we can almost guess. It's like being on the same wavelength. Anyway, to be even mentioned in the same breath as Ryan Moore is an honour and I have the utmost respect for him.

Asfoora was obviously the biggest disappointment today. I just never felt like she got hold of the ground properly but have no idea why. It was a very fast flat five which on paper should have suited her. She just never got any traction. I went into the race brimming with confidence and was sure we'd win. These things happen, though.

I've had a great time down at Richard's so far. Despite what I've been up to at York during the day I've been able to steer most of our conversations towards showjumping. It might get a bit boring for them but it's a big opportunity for me and is one that I can't pass up. Last night the weather was atrocious and when we woke up in the morning the trampoline had been blown from the garden right over our cars. Fortunately it didn't make contact. A showjumping trampoline with a clear round. That's novel.

SATURDAY, 24 AUGUST 2024

Wetherby

Today has been a very good day (one of the best days of the year, in fact) and I couldn't have wished for a better way to round off the Ebor. See The Fire in the Strensall Stakes was as much pressure as a Group 1 really. Andrew doesn't have loads of superstars this year and I wanted to get it right on her. We had a tricky draw though and it was left completely up to me as to how to ride her. It took a bit of balls to come back and follow after giving away a good start, but fortunately when I made the move she was electric. It was a huge relief and hopefully that will set her up for the Prix de l'Opéra at Longchamp on Arc day. Ground isn't too important, so long as it's not super slow. Anyway, let's see. Tropical Storm finally got a win at the fifth attempt in a Listed race against some talented horses. I never moved on him and kept sitting and he actually waited for the others. I saved enough smacks to encourage him late on and when he crossed the line he still had plenty left. He's an exciting horse going forward. Anyway, it's back to Lambourn for me with a big day at Goodwood tomorrow.

MONDAY, 2 SEPTEMBER 2024

Lambourn

Yesterday I went to Longchamp for three Listed races. Only one of my horses stood much of a chance but we got pipped at the post unfortunately. It was a long day, that's for sure. It's fine if you're flying privately but you can't really justify that to the owners with Listed races worth the equivalent of around £23,000 to the winner. Getting the horse there alone will cost them well over £2,000 and a flight for me would be at least £5,000. You just can't do it. The trade-off is that instead of it being a five-hour day for me it's more like a thirteen-hour day, and you're cutting it pretty fine at that. I rode in the 4.35 at Longchamp and managed to catch the 6.15 from Charles de Gaulle back to Heathrow. Only just though. I always use a motorbike rider when I'm in Paris and it's quite an adrenaline rush weaving in and around the traffic.

Unlike my trips to Wolverhampton or Lingfield on a Tuesday evening, which are long but with a high chance of winners, yesterday was more about loyalty. David Menuisier has been good to me over the years and the reward for me going to places like Longchamp for him on a Sunday is that I can ride pretty much any horse I want in the yard. David and I have a very good relationship. He's a good man and an excellent trainer.

I think I'm now forty-seven wins ahead in the championship with six or seven weeks to go. A lot of people have been saying that my lead is unassailable but I never take anything for granted. Last week, for instance, I had the choice of riding two days at Sandown with lots of chances or Bellum Justum in the Nashville Derby Stakes at Kentucky Downs. That race alone was worth the equivalent of over £860,000 to the winner. Even after tax and expenses the winning jockey would come away with about £55,000 which is normally the most amount of prize money I'd ever earn in a month in the UK. In addition to this I'd been riding and working Bellum Justum in the lead-up to the race and he felt great.

Despite the above and despite my lead, I decided that I couldn't afford to miss Sandown. As well as all the chances I mentioned, Tamfana was running in a Group 3 there that I didn't want to miss. Also, what if Bellum Justum didn't travel well or didn't handle the conditions?

Well, what do you think happened? Bellum Justum won handsomely and the jockey got a nice payday. The lucky recipient was none other than Frankie Dettori, which probably won't surprise you. He called me with some questions about the horse a few days before and I told him he was on to a good thing. Had the stakes not been quite as high, Frankie would have ribbed me afterwards but as it was he didn't. Then again, nor did he send me a share of his winnings!

The only bit of good news was that I came away from Sandown with five wins over the two days which put my strike rate up to 24 per cent. Looking back it was a ridiculous decision though. Really daft. I'm not one for regrets but that's driven me pretty damn close. Anyway, let's talk about something else.

OK, what am I looking forward to over the next forty-seven days, which I've just worked out is how long there is left of the season? The meeting up at Doncaster in a couple of weeks has been front and centre over the last few days. That fella Tropical Storm who won at York last month is going to run in the five-furlong race. It's a Group 2 and is called the Flying Childers Stakes. I think he can win that and if he stays healthy he could go to the Breeders' Cup for the Juvenile Sprint. Tom Marquand won both those races on Big Evs last year and Tropical Storm could easily do the same. Here's hoping.

The big question for me with regards to the Doncaster meeting is whether I ride New Century over at Woodbine in Canada for Andrew on the Saturday or whether I ride Sunway for David Menuisier in the St Leger. We're just weighing up how New Century is at the moment before any decisions are made. Unlike Sandown versus Kentucky, this is more about the future than anything else. New Century's is definitely bright and if he does run it's important that I'm on him. Financially, the difference could, once again, be significant. The St Leger is worth £450,000 to the winner whereas the Grade 1 over at Woodbine would be worth £117,000. Even so, Sunway will be up against some seriously strong competition and to be honest with you I don't really fancy his chances. It sounds like I'm being defeatist but I have to follow my head. New Century is as tough and hardy as they come and he tries like crazy which is half the battle. He's also had three races now so he's got some experience.

Something else I'm looking forward to is riding See The Fire in the Prix de l'Opéra on Arc day. It's a race that I'd love to win and I really rate her chances. Speaking of Arc day,

Cool Hoof Luke who won the Gimcrack Stakes at York is likely to go in the Prix Jean-Luc Lagardère. That race used to be a mile but is now seven furlongs and he'd be in the top two or three in the betting. If I ride him behind the leaders, make sure I get cover and make sure he breathes, then I think he's going to improve for going seven furlongs again. We had to come back to six at York last time out because he looked like a non-stayer at Goodwood in July, but we rode him too positively then. He also has the size so as long as he keeps eating he should be improving every month.

The time around the Arc could be very big for me. On Champions Day at Ascot, Tamfana is likely to go for the QEII. A three-year-old getting her ground, doesn't mind soft or heavy. Getting all the weight off the likes of Charyn for Roger Varian that's been doing really well. I fancy her to go very close. In the Qipco Fillies & Mares Stakes, Kalpana could be strong. She won very well at Hamilton which I know was only a Listed race but she will be one of the favourites.

I've only had two Group 1 wins this year so far whereas I had five in total last year. Barring a complete disaster, the championship should be safe, but if I could round things off with another two or three Group 1s I'd be thrilled to bits. See The Fire is the one I'm really hopeful of. Honestly, that would make my year.

Something I've been doing a lot of at the tracks just recently is interacting with young fans. It's obviously been the school holidays so there have been swarms of them. It's a part of the job that I genuinely enjoy. Partly because I simply enjoy meeting them (they're almost always polite and charming), but also because at the end of the day they're the future of the sport. We're always going to play second fiddle to the likes of football and rugby when it comes to young fans and so we should encourage the ones who take an interest, not to mention their families. There's a fella who brings his son to a lot of the meetings. He always makes an effort to come and say hello to me and I always make an effort to stop and have a chat. He's a lovely young man and a real enthusiast.

There's a charity I support that does wonders in this field called Racing to School. It was set up to give children who wouldn't ordinarily get to access horse racing the chance to immerse themselves in the sport and learn all about it. They take them to yards and to tracks. They see the weighing rooms and try on silks, and so forth. It's an amazing organization and they do great work.

Another reason why I enjoy engaging with younger fans and encouraging their enthusiasm is because it isn't that long since I was one myself. Standing on the edge of the parade ring hoping and praying that a jockey might acknowledge me or give me their goggles. Because of my Uncle Jim it used to happen quite a lot so I was lucky in that respect. It didn't make me appreciate it any less though. Every single encounter was a massive thrill.

I remember being shown into the weighing room at Killarney Racecourse aged about twelve. It was the first time I'd ever been in one and the experience was almost spiritual. I'm not joking. It was like visiting some kind of holy sanctuary. I experienced something similar when I went to Ballydoyle for the first time a few years later. A feeling of deep reverence for my surroundings.

My first human version of that, as in a person who I was almost speechless on meeting, was Colm O'Donoghue. He was riding for Aidan when I arrived there and had won a shedload of major races including the Irish Derby, the Prix Jacques Le Marois and the Queen Elizabeth II Challenge Cup Stakes over in Kentucky. He was a genuine international jockey and I couldn't believe that we worked at the same place. He always used to dress very smartly I remember and was a great example to a young pretender like me.

I'm pleased to report that despite the unrelenting workload I've been feeling OK in myself just recently. The therapy has been doing its job and I've been sleeping relatively well. I've already been to Mass this morning and I've got seven rides at Windsor this evening. Tomorrow will be a very early start as I'm riding out for David Menuisier before Goodwood. It's likely I'll have to do 8st 6lb on a filly of Andrew's on Thursday in a sprint at Salisbury. She's my only winning chance of the day and I'd rather put myself through the torture and then ride her than watch somebody else do it. It's a fear of missing out, I suppose. Oh well, it's not forever. My God, imagine if it was!

MONDAY, 9 SEPTEMBER 2024

Somewhere between London and Frome

I hope you're all ready for a shock because I'm actually having a full horse-free day off today. I'm being serious. There has been no riding out and no racing. In fact, recording this is the closest I've come to working all day so far. I went to Mass at 9am, I had counselling at 11am and then I took Lizzy, my girlfriend, for lunch at a restaurant called The Enterprise in Chelsea. I'm now on my way from London to Frome in Somerset where my sister Bláithín lives. My dad's been staying with her for a few days so I'm going to pick them up, take them out for dinner and then drive back to Lambourn. You'd be forgiven for wondering why I'm not just relaxing at home, but I don't get days off very often so when I do I've a lot to fit in. Also, having lunch with Lizzy and seeing my family are things I really look forward to and at the end of the day I'm used to sitting in a car for hours on end.

I don't see my dad anywhere near as much as I'd like to. He's had various health issues over recent years which prevents him from travelling very much. It's obviously the opposite for me which unfortunately curtails our opportunities to meet.

Like me, my dad is also a recovering alcoholic. In fact, I'm fairly sure he turned thirty-five years sober this year which is brilliant. It's left its mark on him though, health-wise, and has contributed greatly to the problems he suffers with today. Despite what he was going through himself, when my sisters and I were kids, my dad always went to great lengths to try and dissuade us from drinking in later life. He wouldn't just lecture us though. He was much more considered than that and at the same time I don't think he was too keen on talking about his own issues. At least not to his three children.

When driving back from Mass or from a pony meeting, he'd sometimes tell us about somebody from his AA group who had fallen off the wagon and gone back on the drink. He'd never name names, of course, nor did he ever finish off the story with a lesson. You know the kind of thing I mean: 'Remember, children; don't let this happen to you.' All he would do is tell us stories of how people he knew had basically ruined their lives through drink.

I suppose you might be thinking, well it didn't do much

good for you, Oisin. In truth, it actually did. Or should I say, it does. Drinking to excess was something I did during an incredibly difficult time in my life, and no amount of previous stories from my dad (or even lectures had there been any) or from anyone else would have prevented me from doing it. The only thing that did eventually stop me drinking was getting caught out and then going into recovery. Now that I'm here, the stories my dad used to tell me resonate greatly and help me when times are tough. Also, if I ever did want to talk to him about it, the door would always be open. My approach to recovery is simple. I make a promise to myself at the start of each day that I won't drink and each time I fulfil that promise I glean a tiny amount of strength.

I had a good chat with Steve Hamilton, the man who does my garden, this morning. He belongs to a racing syndicate and their horse ran at Brighton earlier today and won. He's called Mirabeau and although it finished up at 6/1, the lads managed to get their money on at about 33/1. They all had a good few quid on apparently so they must have won a small fortune. I hope they did. There were a few non-runners in the race but who cares. A win's a win.

Tomorrow morning I'm going to be riding out for Richard Hughes before going to Lingfield where I've got some decent rides. Hughesy is just down the road so instead of having to get up at 5am, which is what happens when I'm riding out for David Menuisier, I can have a bit of a lie-in. Well, until at least 6am.

Racing-wise, my potential big dilemma at the moment is that Kalpana and Queen Of The Pride might both be running in the Fillies and Mares on Qipco British Champions Day. I've no idea which one I'll partner if that's the case but

as Queen Of The Pride is owned by Sheikh Fahad it'll probably be her. In addition to this, Tamfana, whom I won the
Group 3 on at Sandown, could run in the Sun Chariot at
Newmarket which will now clash with the Qatar Prix Jean-
Luc Lagardère at Longchamp. It'll either be Cool Hoof Luke
in that race or Tamfana in the Sun Chariot. You can't plan
too much in advance because as we know, horses can go
lame or become ill, so you have to sit tight and make an
informed decision as late as you possibly can. It's not a bad
problem to have in some respects but it can play on your
mind a bit. Well, it can play on my mind, that's for sure.

This coming weekend is very important. Particularly
Sunday which is the Irish St Leger. I've got Giavellotto for
Marco Botti and I hope the ground stays good or faster.
His form at Newmarket (he won there with a 3lb penalty
for winning The Yorkshire Cup at York) hasn't been franked
because the second horse, Arrest, failed to win in France.
(Basically the form of a race is 'franked' when the placed
horses go on to run well in subsequent races, meaning the
value of the performance is therefore potentially enhanced.)
It's very hard to win a Group race with a penalty but he did.
The biggest danger will be Kyprios. He'll be favourite but
Giavellotto is the faster horse, particularly over a mile and
six. Ballydoyle will make sure there's a strong tempo, but
Giavellotto has been trained specifically for this race so let's
hope it stays dry.

On Saturday I'm riding New Century over at Woodbine in
Canada. This obviously means I miss the St Leger at Doncaster but it's my biggest Group 1 chance in a while and I have
to take it. Al Qudra is in there who's already beaten New
Century this year and will be favourite, but New Century

is improving all the time. As I've already mentioned, a mile would suit him but he's a horse that I think will suit ten furlongs next year. Whether he's good enough to beat Al Qudra I don't know. It's a big field with fourteen of them. It's normally smaller but some might scratch (become non-runners). One thing I'm sure of is that the European horses will be too good for the Americans. European turf horses tend to dominate against American turf horses as in Europe we breed them specifically for turf races, whereas in America they tend to breed them to race on dirt.

OK, I've had enough of the sound of my own voice now. I'm going to enjoy the rest of my day off.

WEDNESDAY, 18 SEPTEMBER 2024

En route from Sandown to Lambourn

I'm just on my way back home from Sandown where I had one winner on a horse I rode out about six months ago for Harry Charlton called Cosmic Year. I didn't actually get much sleep last night because I was thinking about him. I remember saying to Harry after that work I did that he could be quite special. I hadn't seen him since, until today, and what kept me up last night was wondering what he might be like. What if I was mistaken about his promise, etc.? Before a big race I don't have this kind of issue because nine times out of ten I'll know the horse I'm riding well so will know what to expect, within reason. When they fall into this category, and it's rare for me, it really occupies my mind. The lack of sleep obviously isn't ideal but being kept awake by anticipation and excitement once in a while isn't such a bad thing. After all, it's one of the reasons why I became a jockey in the first place. He's one of the most exciting horses I've ridden in a very long time so fingers crossed he has progressed since our last meeting.

I sold a yearling that I own half of at Keeneland in Kentucky last week for $310,000. I bought the mare after the Breeders' Cup Classic in 2018. Apart from one of her progeny dying, most have done very well. The fellas that sold her for me are Irish, Adrian Regan and Fergus Galvin, and they do a great job. They thought she'd make over $200,000 so the fact that she made over $300,000 is tremendous. I've already stated that I wouldn't have what it takes to buy and sell horses for a living, but when something like this happens it drives me on and makes me question things. A few minutes later, after I've reminded myself of all the crap they go through, I come back down to earth and get on with being a jockey again.

I'm very, very happy to report that New Century won over at Woodbine last Saturday. That makes it three Group 1 wins for the season which to be honest isn't a brilliant number. If I could win another two or three I'd be a heck of a lot happier. To finish a season having not won the Jockeys Championship would be a disappointment, but to finish one having not won a Group 1 would be a personal and professional disaster. It'd be an enormous disappointment.

At the risk of repeating myself, I'm pinning my hopes for an improvement on that number with Kalpana, who will have a great chance in the Fillies and Mares at Ascot on Champions Day, as well as Tamfana in the Sun Chariot Stakes at Newmarket, See The Fire in the Prix de l'Opéra and Cool Hoof Luke in the aforementioned Prix Jean-Luc

Lagardère. All four would be a dream come true but I'd be happy with one.

The performance by New Century at Woodbine was incredibly gutsy, especially when you consider the fact that he'd had to travel to Canada via Kentucky. Why that was the case I'm not entirely sure, but getting him there in such good order was a hell of a job so well done to all those involved. What pleases me the most, of course, is that he's improved enough to win a Group 1. I stated before he ever ran that I thought he had a big future. It's a bit of a disappointment when you get it wrong about a horse but when you get it right it's tremendous.

Thinking about it, he might actually end up being my last chance of a Group 1 this year as he'll go in the Breeders' Cup Juvenile at the start of November. The track at Del Mar will be sharp enough for him but it'll be a different sort of track to Woodbine. The straight is much shorter (about 200 metres) which won't play to his strengths, but he's had an experience going around a turn now and he took everything in his stride. That should stand him in good stead against the horses that are coming over from the UK and Ireland.

It's been a real mixed bag for me over the past week or so and emotionally I've taken a hammering. I got on the scoresheet in the first race at Doncaster last Thursday but then had thirteen losers over the next two days. That was very hard to take. I try and remind myself that it's just the nature of the beast but sometimes it makes no difference.

On Saturday I had to get on a plane to Canada knowing that I had weight to lose, but it was delayed by two hours. They made up time in the air fortunately and I arrived at Woodbine roughly two and a half hours before my first ride.

I hadn't eaten that day but was straight in the sauna for forty-five minutes. I wasn't feeling that great to be honest with you but William Buick was in there with me and we chatted away about horses and the day ahead. William is incredibly knowledgeable so when we're in that situation time tends to fly.

My relationship with William has been quite fractious over the years, although over the last twelve months or so we've got on very well. This was mainly due to the fact we were both so competitive. He was going for the championship, as was I, and each of us were competing for a lot of the same rides.

William is the most perfect rider to watch on a horse. He's got great balance, good hands, is fantastic in a finish and has a great racing brain. He can also do the same weights as me and is still very hungry despite his success and despite now being a big family man. There's a mutual respect between us that I want to keep because I truly admire him.

With James Doyle, who is my other main competitor when it comes to picking up spare rides, things are a bit more straightforward. James and I have always got on very well and I wouldn't be afraid to pick up the phone to him anytime. While I was suspended he was very good to me. Due mainly to the size of my mortgage I didn't have a lot of spare cash when I couldn't ride and whenever we went to the boxing together or for meals he would always insist on paying. He's a true gentleman.

James also struggles with his weight but he's an achiever. As a young man he had high-pressure rides on Kingman for Juddmonte but he handled it all incredibly well. Eight years later in 2022 he won on Cachet for George Boughey in the Qipco 1,000 Guineas and then the Qipco 2,000 on Coroebus for Charlie Appleby and Godolphin the following day. That's the standard of rider he is. Away from the track, James is a great judge from work. In fact, he's probably the best I know. Just ask the aforementioned Charlie Appleby. When James said something about a horse he trusted him implicitly.

I'm often asked by people what it takes to become a top jockey and to be honest with you it isn't one of my favourite questions. Not least because it's so incredibly difficult to answer. It's an amalgamation of many things I think. Many different qualities and facets. If I had to pick one, however, that sets top jockeys apart from the rest of the field, it would have to be their ability to compartmentalize things and keep a clear head. Now I'll have to explain myself. In short, when everything has been going down the toilet and they're in a state of despair, these people are able to put it all to one side in a split second, recalibrate and, as they walk into the paddock for the next race, make themselves and those around them believe that they are the best in the world. Not only that, they also then have to ride like they're the best in the world. That, in my opinion, is one of the main things that separates top jockeys from the rest. And believe me, it's not easy. You remember at the very start of the book I talked about giving off an air of good humour regardless of how I was feeling. Well, that's part and parcel of what I'm talking about. You have to actually believe it though. You have to live it. It's no use just putting on a smile and saying, 'I'm fine'.

I'll tell you what, I have a much better example.

I'm going to take you back to Royal Ascot in 2021. I knew the BHA were after me for going to Mykonos the previous September during Covid and I knew that I was going to be handed a suspension. I just didn't know for how long.

Subsequently, my approach to Royal Ascot that year was that it might just be my last race meeting of the season and by the time the Commonwealth Cup came around on the Friday I had four winners to my name and was in front in the race to be leading rider at Royal Ascot. My ride in the Commonwealth Cup was the horse I mentioned earlier called Dragon Symbol.

Dragon Symbol's journey to this point had been an eventful one as after arriving in England after the sale he fractured his pelvis almost immediately which meant I couldn't sell him. After he recovered I sent him to Archie Watson and he won his first four races. I had a feeling that Dragon Symbol would win the Commonwealth Cup and I was right. In the stewards' room afterwards, however, the win was taken off me for careless riding. Both Dragon Symbol under me and Lady Aurelia under Frankie Dettori drifted off a line on very slow ground. Frankie didn't think he'd get the race but the stewards decided to give it to him. It was live on ITV and was very, very hard to take. I was incandescent with rage.

Thirty-five minutes after leaving the stewards' office I had to ride the somewhat ironically named Alcohol Free in the Coronation Cup. Ironically named because I was about to be suspended, partly for having failed two blood tests for alcohol, yet had managed not to drink at all in the week leading up to the meeting. I was still raging inside about what had happened just a few minutes earlier but for the time being I had to put it to one side. Not just partly, but completely.

Shortly before the race the heavens began to open which changed, not only the ground, but how I would approach the race. I walked into the parade ring and told Andrew and Anna Lisa Balding and the owner Jeff Smith what I was going to do, mounted Alcohol Free and cantered her down to the start. I could still feel the rage bubbling under but there was no way in the world I could allow it to manifest itself. I had a job to do on Alcohol Free and if anything the incident before had made me even more determined to win.

The start of the race went as planned and I immediately got the position I wanted which was directly behind the favourite, Pretty Gorgeous. Then, at the bottom of the straight when everyone else was starting to move and ask for some effort, I sat still and allowed her to fill up for the next ten strides or so. When I picked her up she took off like a rocket and we led from a furlong out. As we crossed the line I stuck my tongue out in defiance to the stewards who had taken the Commonwealth Cup off me, but that's the only time I allowed what had happened earlier to get the better of me. It's actually uncharacteristic of me to do something like that but I forgave myself that one.

Despite claiming that top jockeys are able to compartmentalize things like that (and they are), I'm not sure how I managed to get through that one. In addition to the Dragon Symbol debacle beforehand I was also carrying the pressure of knowing that I was facing a lengthy ban. It came from somewhere though.

While we're on the subject of top jockeys, it would be remiss of me not to offer you a few thoughts on some of my other peers and contemporaries in the weighing room.

I'm known for being quite forensic in my approach to what we do for a living but I'm not the only one. Dan Muscutt and Billy Loughnane carry little books around with them in which they write down information on every horse they ride. They then refer back to this information when they ride them again. It's a good system and is something I should try doing myself.

When I started out, the older jockeys such as Richard Hughes and Kieren Fallon were far busier than the rest of us and that was basically because they were the best. All of us had some talent but they were in a completely different league. Thanks partly to their brilliance, the general standard of jockey is very high these days. The likes of Tom Marquand, Rossa Ryan, David Egan, Hollie Doyle, Clifford Lee, Jason Watson, Callum Rodriguez, Kieran Shoemark and Rob Hornby, to name but a few. These guys are only in their twenties yet they all ride at a very high level.

It's my belief that there is more talent in the British weighing room than anywhere else on earth at the moment. You have Ryan Moore at the very top of the tree. He's showing no signs of slipping and it's important to the likes of William, James Doyle and me that he doesn't. Having younger talent nipping at your heels is a great motivator but so is having somebody great to aspire to.

What's really heartening is that the aforementioned youngsters are only going to get better and better. They're all very strong and switched on but they're also approachable and know how to communicate. As importantly, they all have a following these days which is becoming more and more important. Billy Loughnane is just eighteen years of age. I've never seen an eighteen-year-old ride as well as him. He is a little bit big so his weight might be a problem in the future. He's way beyond his years though. A truly prodigious talent.

Tom Marquand has a great way about him. He doesn't get too wrapped up in it all yet he's always incredibly focused. And talented, of course. He's the opposite to me in that I live, breathe and dream racing 24/7, and the consequences of that are the highs and lows I have to deal with. It's often the same when you get too close to something. Tom's ability to bring the same attitude to the job but to be able to walk away from it at the end of the day is enviable.

OK, back to wasting at Woodbine.

There was a bath at the track which looked incredibly complicated to operate so I asked my valet to fill it for me. When he did he made it too hot (anything over 40 degrees is dangerous) which meant I had to add ice to get it down to below that. I sat in that for an hour and when I got out I was 8st 5½. I had two 8st 8lbs and one 8st 10lb so I did it pretty easily in the end.

I got a night flight back to London after the race and landed at Heathrow at 9.30am having not really slept. The small plane that was due to take me straight to Ireland for the Irish St Leger meeting had a mechanical failure so I ended up going over on my cousins' plane – William and Wolan Byrne – at the last minute. I had to wait an hour and a half and so missed my first two rides at the Curragh. In the big race, Giavellotto got hot on the way to the start and unfortunately he underperformed. It's usually not a complex business getting to the start, but at the Curragh you've got to go over the plains to get to the one mile six furlong start and on this occasion it just fried his head. I found that very frustrating.

On Monday at Windsor I had seven ordinary horses and won on just one of them which isn't a good enough strike rate. Yesterday at Yarmouth things turned around for me. I had two for Saeed bin Suroor and came away with both. We've got an excellent strike rate together and I'm glad I was able to maintain it.

It's all racing at the moment. I met a friend, Fred Milne, for a coffee earlier and he made the assumption that as it's September, things must be calming down a bit. 'You must be able to take your foot off the gas,' he said. 'You're joking,' I replied. I then showed him my diary. 'Bloody hell, so there really is no let-up then,' he said. 'No, not until the end of October.'

Yesterday I spent a total of eight and a half hours in the car before and after riding seven at Yarmouth and I went to bed at 11pm but couldn't sleep because of Cosmic Year. During long journeys I tend not to converse with my driver very much. For a start, I obviously want to leave him alone to drive, but because we spend so much time in each other's company it could easily become a case of familiarity breeding contempt. It's a professional relationship at the end of the day and for the sake of its longevity it has to be looked after.

As well as keeping myself up to date with form and the like, which is obviously essential, I spend a lot of time looking at pedigrees. Knowledge is power but I've an enormous thirst for it which helps. Eventually I will get bored of the horse-related stuff and when that happens I'll start looking at world news. This interests me a lot at the moment and there is plenty going on to hold my attention. Because I'm quite inquisitive I tend to research a lot of the people I come across in the articles I read so it's a similar approach to racing really. The more I know, the happier I am. This is also a good leveller as it reminds me that there are more important things going on in the world than horses running around grass fields with people on the back of them.

I was up at 5.30am this morning to go to Andrew's where

I rode work on See The Fire and Royal Playwright who are actually half-siblings. I then went to Kempton and galloped Kikkuli, Frankel's half-brother, for Harry Charlton, and I've just ridden six at Sandown. Then tomorrow it's Yarmouth again. It's just relentless. Or at least it feels relentless.

Please don't think I'm moaning, by the way. I promise you I'm not. I'm just venting. In fact, I'm in a much better position than a lot of my fellow jockeys. If I decided to give it all up tomorrow I'd have enough money in the bank to keep me going for a while and would have plenty of opportunities for alternative employment, whether that be dabbling in buying and selling horses or working in the media. I'd be OK. The vast majority of jockeys wouldn't have that luxury which is one of the reasons why I talk about the workload so much. I want people to appreciate just how intense and abnormal our existence is, in the hope that people might actually cut us some slack when they're laying into us on social media. We do it because we love it but we also do it because it earns us a living and without us there wouldn't be a sport.

The big news over the past week, apart from winning on New Century, is that I lost my temper big time with the stewards at Haydock the other day. I was called in for a stewards' enquiry after a one-mile-six-furlong race for allegedly having caused interference into the first turn and was given a two-day ban for careless riding. What made me so angry on this occasion wasn't actually the suspension (although I did find it unjust), it was the language that the stewards used to describe what happened. They said that because of the way I had ridden, the other riders involved, Joe Fanning and Rossa Ryan, had been forced to take evasive action and that Rossa Ryan had become unbalanced. For a start, the bend at Haydock is extremely sharp and I knew for a fact that I'd done everything in my power to take it safely. Ergo, I had not ridden carelessly.

After hearing their full description of the event, which as I said I found exaggerated and inflammatory, I saw red and called it a disgrace. I didn't use any foul language but I was absolutely fuming. One of the stewards there (somebody whom I actually respect) then took me out of the room and told me not to worry about it. 'You're too good to get stressed out over these sorts of things,' he said. I appreciated what he said and got the feeling that he hadn't been in agreement with either the decision or the description. I can't say for sure, of course. He just seemed very empathetic. It takes a lot for me to lose my temper like that, especially with stewards, and I would only ever do so if I genuinely believed that I'd been treated very unfairly.

Sometimes it can go either way with a stewards' enquiry and when that's the case, although I might end up being disappointed, I'm big enough and mature enough to bite my lip and just move on. It's a jury system after all which means it's subjective and because it's subjective, mistakes can be made and sometimes are.

In order for the system to work as well as it can, you obviously have to minimize the chances of mistakes being made. A starting point to achieving this would be maximizing the knowledge, expertise and experience of the stewards. This, in my humble opinion, is where the BHA are lacking somewhat, although I have to say that it has been improving over recent years. The vast majority of people who judge our performances on the track have never ridden a horse in a competitive environment, least of all a thoroughbred. Nor could they ever appreciate any of the extenuating circumstances that might exist. Knowledge is obviously important but if your opinion is potentially going to affect somebody's career, then that opinion needs to be based at least partly on experience. In my opinion.

There's a big argument going on in Formula 1 at the moment, which I follow a bit, that race stewards should be professionals, as in paid professionals. A lot of these people are already former drivers, which makes sense, but because they're volunteers and only attend certain races, the current system is lacking in both consistency and cohesion. The permutations that might exist when making a judgement on something arising in such a complicated and technical sport as Formula 1 are almost infinite, which makes a part-time volunteer stewarding system inadequate at best and at worst laughable. It's one of the richest sports in the world yet it cannot see the value in having full-time professional stewards passing judgement on their drivers and teams. That's just bizarre.

Do you remember when football referees became professionals? I was only very young when it happened but I've read enough literature since then to know that the difference was immediate. Referees had always been a bit untouchable whereas now they were culpable. And what happened? The standard of refereeing went up. I'm not saying the system is perfect but it's a lot better than it used to be in the so-called good old days.

If I could change one thing about the current race day penal system that exists within horse racing, apart from the above, it would be to penalize transgressions such as minor careless riding incidents and minor whip infringements with fines instead of bans.

As a result of the suspension I got at Haydock, I ended up losing out on two winners which, had things been different, could have cost me the championship. You shouldn't have a situation in a major sport where one of its protagonists could potentially lose a championship because of a minor careless riding incident (that at the end of the day is subjective and has not been adjudicated by people with direct experience) or because they've accidentally gone one over on the whip. You can hit a horse one too many times by mistake and if that race is worth more than £50,000, regardless of where you finish, you will receive an immediate four-day ban. It's almost as if they're willing us to fail. It's nonsensical.

Richard Hughes tried to get this changed a few years ago and stopped riding but it didn't make any difference. In order for something like that to stick you'd need the backing of every jockey in the country and there are too many who don't want to rock the boat. Understandably so.

Not only would a fine be much fairer by not interfering with or damaging someone's career, but it would generate money for the sport. I appreciate that I'm commenting as somebody who would be able to afford these fines, but if a jockey couldn't afford it then why not give them a choice. Take a fine or take a ban. For dangerous and improper riding, suspensions are obviously justified, but in order to create more of a deterrent you could combine them with a fine.

Anyway, I'd better shut my mouth before I get myself into trouble, if I haven't done so already. I should probably take more heed of the saying Davy Russell taught me: 'A closed mouth catches no flies.'

SEVEN

Champions Day

WEDNESDAY, 25 SEPTEMBER 2024

Lambourn

LAST SATURDAY WAS ONE OF those days that makes you happy to be alive and me even happier that I chose to become a jockey. I had four races at Newbury and came away with three wins, although that wasn't the reason for my euphoria. While cantering to post it felt like I really got inside the horses' heads and made them listen to me. I try and do the same thing with every horse I ride, but I only sense a connection like that very, very occasionally. For it to happen three times in a day is just unheard of.

I dare say there'll be one or two people nodding their heads in recognition at reading this, but there'll be a whole lot more who think it's bonkers. The thing is that unless you experience something like that first-hand, it's incredibly hard to explain. Horses are very sensitive creatures but they're also very astute and intelligent and there are more things we don't know about them than do. For all my talk

197

of winning and being competitive, experiences like that are what make me love working with horses. I'm still buzzing.

Anyway, after the euphoria came the relief as the three wins helped to bump up my strike rate for September which so far had been poor. I'm still well over forty wins ahead but it doesn't make any difference. Until the presentation takes place at Ascot and I'm handed the trophy, I'll not be able to rest properly.

On Sunday I had the first of what unintentionally became three uninterrupted days off, as in no riding out or racing. I can't remember the last time that happened. In March when I had the suspension I rode breeze-up horses in Ireland. Honestly, it must have been during the fourteen-month ban. Anyway, it's been enjoyable. Although I must admit I'm starting to suffer a bit from withdrawal symptoms.

I always intended to have Sunday off but then the Leicester meeting got rained off on Monday and so that was that. Sometimes when I suddenly have a day to myself, I'll panic slightly as I'm not used to having nothing to do. That usually lasts about five minutes which is how long it takes for the day to fill up. In this case I decided to drive up to Leicestershire anyway and visit my Uncle Jim whom I hadn't seen in ages. We ended up going cubbing together which is a term used for training young foxhounds. It normally takes place either early evening or very early in the morning when the scent is strong and in addition to training the young foxhounds it helps to get the horses fit. It's not a very exciting thing to do but my Uncle Jim is big into hunting and it was nice to spend time with him. He, more than anyone else I'm close to, understands every element of what I go through as a jockey and I can tell him anything. He's a good listener too, which helps.

I also enjoy hunting but my interest is restricted really to jumping and running fast at things. It's the danger element basically. I get a good buzz from hitting the ground at speed. I've had a few falls over the years (nothing serious fortunately) but falling during a hunt is very different to falling during a race. You're obviously not immune to injury but the ground is usually soft and you're normally riding through big open fields. Most importantly, though, you don't have ten other horses riding directly behind and around you. That's the big difference.

On one very memorable day last season I was sitting at the top of a hill and there was a huge hedge at the bottom of it. I went down the hill as fast as my horse was comfortable going (it probably wasn't very fast as I was on a cob-type horse) but as well as clearing the hedge we must have landed ten metres the other side. It was a huge thrill. I want to say it jumped perfectly, but we hit the deck. That's where I got the thrill. Fortunately, I wasn't hurt!

Yesterday I went up to London as I had an appointment with my dentist. I stayed in Knightsbridge but decided to walk the five miles to the surgery. As I hadn't ridden for a few days I was concerned that I might be a little bit heavy but I needn't have worried. I was 8st 10lb this morning after riding work for Andrew and have 8st 9lb to make later so I didn't blow up too much.

MONDAY, 30 SEPTEMBER

En route to London

I'm on my way to the Indian Consulate in London. There are actually two in the capital, one on Aldwych which is at the top of the Strand and one in Islington, and unfortunately I have to go to the one in Islington. No offence to anyone who lives there but it's a far bigger pain in the backside to get to than the one in Aldwych. I'll be having a few days in India this side of Christmas at a meeting so I need to sort out my visa. I also have two trips to South Africa coming up at the end of November and January which I'm looking forward to. Depending on what's happening I might just stay on there for a few days during the second trip and have a holiday. People assume that because I visit lots of different countries I must get to see a lot of interesting things. If only. In the vast majority of cases my itinerary for a trip abroad will look like this:

Home » Airport » Plane » Airport » Hotel » Track » Hotel » Track » Airport » Plane » Airport » Home.

And that's if I'm staying overnight. If I'm not I'll go from the track to the airport and straight home again. It's not that I don't want to stay in these places and see what they have to offer. It's just down to the schedule. Every jockey is in the same situation, whether it's domestic or international. There is so much racing these days and the fact is that if you don't ride a horse somebody else will.

I was supposed to be riding at Windsor later on today but it's been called off. I can't say I'm too disappointed, although when I heard, my immediate reaction was to find out whether Tom and Rossa were riding anywhere else. It only lasted a split second as I knew they weren't but I must have forgotten momentarily.

My driver is off at the moment and so I'm having to drive myself. It's very much a first-world problem, of course, but yesterday was tough and I had a dreadful night's sleep. I had five rides at Epsom and they were all pretty revved up going to post with hoods on and what have you. Every jockey on the planet will be able to empathize with that. In fact, we should get a double riding fee for some of them. Epsom's probably the worst track for that. As well as tens of thousands of people all making a noise, you have a big funfair right in the middle of the track. It's a lot for a horse to take in and subsequently, a lot of them need to wear hoods.

By the time I got home I was about as wound up as the horses had been at the track and found it hard to come down. I knew I'd have difficulty sleeping and sure enough I was right. What made matters worse was that the entries are due out for Arc weekend as well as the Sun Chariot at Newmarket. If I had my way I'd ride Tamfana in the Sun Chariot on Saturday and Running Lion in the Opera on Sunday. There's chat about Running Lion going to America for the Breeders' Cup Fillies and Mares which is eleven furlongs. This would be a bad idea in my opinion. First, I don't think she'd stay, second, I think the track will be too sharp, third, the ground will be too fast for her and four, she doesn't travel well. When she went over to France for the Prix de Diane in 2023 it took her ages to get over it and she ran terribly. A trip to America would be an expensive mistake in my opinion. Anyway, it's not up to me, thank heaven.

How a bad night's sleep affects me the following day is partly down to the attitude I bring to the situation. For instance, if I tell myself that I'm going to feel like crap after a bad night's sleep then I probably will, whereas if I tell myself that it's happened a thousand times before and that nobody died, which is the reality of the situation, then I'll at least stand a chance of having a decent day. It's never actually that simple, of course. Partly because I have a thousand and one other things going on in my head and partly because I don't always realize it's happening.

WEDNESDAY, 9 OCTOBER 2024

Lambourn

Well, there's a lot to report on and unfortunately none of it is very positive. Sorry, that's not true. Of course positive things have happened and are happening. It's just that some of the negative things have been quite impactful and have been front and centre of my consciousness.

As you know I had Sunway in the Arc for Sheikh Fahad. Although he has a big engine he's more of a stayer these days and was never really in the race. Given the choice of riding a big-priced outsider like that or nothing at all in such a prestigious race you'd obviously choose the former. I really would like to win it one day. It has so much international appeal and recognition. Winning the Arc is like winning the Derby though. Everything needs to come together. You need the perfect ride and the perfect race.

Running Lion ran much better in the Prix de l'Opéra but we could only manage second unfortunately. She actually got the perfect trip and although she chased the winner all the way up the straight she just wasn't quite good enough. It was a fine effort though and it was good to get some Group 1 black type with her (finishing second makes her more valuable).

The biggest disappointment of the weekend was missing out on the Sun Chariot on Saturday. I was obviously hoping to ride Tamfana who ended up winning it but ended up on See The Fire instead, who didn't. To be fair, I was always committed to ride See The Fire but never thought that she'd take on Tamfana. A mile was always going to be too sharp for her (particularly on that track) bearing in mind she wanted every yard of a mile and a furlong at York last time out.

When the decision was made that she would race in the Sun Chariot I knew exactly how it would pan out. Tamfana led from two furlongs out and ran on well whereas See The Fire lost position two furlongs out but then rallied at the end and finished third. David Bowe, who is Jeff Smith's racing and stud manager, and Andrew both apologized to me afterwards but there was no need. I was extremely disappointed but only because I always want to win. Sometimes these things fall in your favour and sometimes they don't. Thanks to Jeff, David and Andrew, I had the link-up with Alcohol Free when I came back from my first suspension and they've always allowed me to ride any horses I want. They don't owe me a thing, least of all an apology.

I was at the Gosdens' this morning to ride Queen Of The Pride who is now going to be running in the Fillies and Mares on Champions Day at Ascot. This is the same race that Kalpana will be running in so it looks like history might be about to repeat itself. Kalpana will be 5/2 favourite and Queen Of The Pride will be 12/1, but because Sheikh Fahad owns Queen Of The Pride I'll be riding her. Listen, it is what it is and we won't complain about it. Seeing Ryan Moore miss out on two Group 1 wins at the weekend because Christophe Soumillon won on two Ballydoyle second strings reminded me that you just have to get over these things. Obviously there's a big difference between Ryan and me – he's won over two hundred Group 1s whereas I've only won thirty-one – but the effect is exactly the same. In fact, he and I have talked about this on one or two occasions and although our initial reactions might appear extreme from time to time, we calm down in seconds. If you don't get upset by something like that then you shouldn't be a jockey, but the same applies if you let it get under your skin. Take what you can from it and then move on.

The championship is all but over now. It doesn't finish officially until the third Saturday in October, but unless the BHA decide to slap a ban on me from now until then and then strip me of fifty wins and award them to Rossa Ryan, I should be home and dry. I've already said that I won't take anything for granted but the fact is that I am about to become a four-time champion jockey. How does that make me feel? To be honest, I don't feel anything really, not at the moment. I don't have time. When I arrive at Ascot on 19 October it might be different, but until then there are too many distractions.

Because I have such a shocking memory (apart from horses' pedigrees and languages) I don't remember a great deal about the first time I lifted the trophy. I got driven around the parade ring in a sports car, which was fun, and I got a nice round of applause when I was introduced to the public. All I remember in any detail about the day is how physically and mentally exhausted I was. And it wasn't as if I could then take a break and appreciate it. I had a full week of racing to look forward to straight after, followed by another and then another. Whatever we might achieve as jockeys, due to the fact that racing is now omnipresent we rarely get a chance to appreciate it.

The presentation itself on Champions Day is quite understated, certainly in comparison to other sporting trophy presentations. In Formula 1 you get magnums of champagne and a blast of 'Les Toreadors' from the opera *Carmen* by Georges Bizet just for winning a Grand Prix. Not that I'll be wanting any champagne this year. Our presentations are a little bit more dignified than that which suits me down to the ground.

Part way through the day, an announcement will be made over the tannoy system that the presentation is going to take place at such and such a time and then those who want to see it turn up and those who do not will stay in the bar. After getting the trophy I might say a few words and that'll be that. It doesn't drag on too long, fortunately.

The big question when I do lift the trophy will be whether or not I want to go for a fifth title. That's the question that the press and public will be asking me and it's one I've been asking myself a lot over the past week or two. Do I want to put myself through all that again? The pain and the sacrifice. I mean, what would be the point? Nobody's ever going to break Gordon Richards' record (he won it twenty-six times) and it's not as if there's a huge pot of gold at the end when you do win the championship. If there was, things might be different, but there isn't. So, what's the motivation? The good thing is I'll have plenty of time to think about it. I don't intend to leave it too long, though. If I decide not to go for the championship in 2025 I'll want as much time as possible to plan an alternative route.

After the disappointment of 2023, the only way I could approach the championship this year was by doing more than everyone else. A lot more. So far I've ridden in over a hundred more races than the two jockeys closest to me, Rossa Ryan and Tom Marquand, and whereas their strike rates are currently 16 per cent and 17 per cent respectively, mine is 22 per cent. Doing the same as everyone else just isn't an option for me so if I did decide to go for a fifth title it would have to be on exactly the same terms. Everything and more or nothing at all. That's the deal.

A couple of weeks ago I had come to the conclusion that I was done with chasing championships but at the moment I'm not so sure. Winning is addictive and this year in particular, winning races has been my lifeblood. It might have something to do with proving myself after the ban, or the disappointment of coming second last year. I don't know. It also isn't a heart versus head thing either. They both want the lot: championships, Group races, Classics. Then again, they also want a bit of sleep and some peace and quiet occasionally.

One thing I do know but which doesn't help me much is that missing out on the Group 1s this year has been really hard to take. I've tried not to think about it too deeply as if I did I could probably identify at least one or two more instances where, had I not been chasing winners all the time, I could have won a Group race. There are two or three that I'm aware of but there could be one or two more. It's all been for the greater good with regards to maintaining the status quo, but now that I've overtaken Ryan and Frankie in championships, surely the ambition going forward has to be quality? Those two are the benchmark after all. The best there's been in a very long time. I wish it was an easy choice.

MONDAY, 14 OCTOBER 2024

Lambourn

Yesterday I passed two hundred winners for the year which isn't bad going. I knew it had been creeping up on me but it came as a bit of a shock when I found out. It sounds a bit blasé, I suppose, but it isn't meant to. My three main obsessions this year in order of how much thought time they've taken up have been the championship, my strike rate and winning as many Group races as possible. I simply haven't had room for any others.

When I set off to Goodwood yesterday I was aware of the fact that I was on 199 wins for the year, but again it wasn't front and centre. Even after the race (I won a six-furlong novices race on a horse called Qetaifan by Starspangledbanner for Andrew) it didn't really hit home. I was feeling a bit lethargic and my mind was elsewhere. It was only when I was walking around the horse sales at Newmarket this morning that it began to hit home properly. From the moment I arrived, people started congratulating me and saying how well I'd done. I'm usually not very good at taking compliments but this was really gratifying. If other people such as racegoers didn't get some kind of gratification from jockeys doing well and winning races, the attraction wouldn't be anywhere near as strong. The glory, statistics and trophies will always belong to you but the euphoria that success brings is for all to share.

Andrew also said some very nice things about me to the media after the race that I read on the way back home from

Newmarket. Andrew doesn't say a lot to the press and media so when he does it's usually because he feels strongly about something. I'm paraphrasing slightly but he said something along the lines of, 'It's a great achievement by Oisin and the fact he's been able to ride that many winners at the better meetings is quite something and I'm delighted he's done so well.' Thanks, boss.

The best year I've had in Britain so far in terms of winners is 226 in 2019. I doubt very much that I'll surpass that this year as after this weekend my agent will be taking fewer rides for me. Even I don't feel tempted to try and top it. It'd be ridiculous. It might still happen though if I have a good October and November. My main priority at the moment is riding at as high a level as possible in the lead-up to the Breeders' Cup meeting. That's actually my new obsession at the moment. I really want to achieve something there.

SATURDAY, 19 OCTOBER 2024

En route from Ascot to Lambourn

I'm just leaving Ascot after what has been an enjoyable but also a very frenetic Champions Day. It's been a frenetic end of the week really. Last night, Qipco held their annual dinner at St James's Palace which was a late night. This is basically a who's who of the upper echelons of British and Irish racing, from Chris Richardson from Cheveley Park Stud and representatives from Coolmore, whether it be M V Magnier or one of his senior employees, to the Gosdens, Anthony Oppenheimer, Sheikh Fahad, Sheik Hamad and Andrew Lloyd Webber. It's a very opulent affair but given the importance of the following day, I always try to leave as quickly and quietly as I can.

Even in my drinking days I would always have done the same. Many choose not to but they don't have to ride five or six horses the following day, or in my case also collect a trophy and have to speak in public. The atmosphere was very upbeat at the dinner and everyone was very congratulatory.

Although I arrived home fairly late last night, I slept well and when I woke up this morning the sun was shining and the birds were singing. It was pretty idyllic. Just like millions of other people, the weather can have a big say in how I feel generally so the fact that the sun was shining today of all days set things up perfectly. It was just the start I needed.

When I arrived at the track I was greeted by members of the press and media who obviously wanted a chat before the day began. Despite what I've said in here about my experiences with the press and media, I should point out that I have a pretty good relationship with a few people within both of these industries and between them they tend to make things just about bearable. I was also feeling quite cheerful this morning which made it easier to ignore the ones I don't care for.

One of the most pleasing things about Champions Day this year was the reaction I received from the staff at Ascot. From the moment I arrived this morning until the moment I left a few minutes ago, every single person I came into contact with either shook my hand or gave me a pat on the back and congratulated me. They were all so genuine and it helped to maintain my mood throughout the entire day. 'I can't wait to watch you pick up the trophy,' one fella said to me as I arrived. 'It's going to be a great moment.'

Ever since I started working as a jockey I have always had

a deep appreciation for the people who work the tracks and I've always gone out of my way to say hello and be polite to them. Perhaps that's why they're always so kind to me? And they are always kind. For as long as I can remember I have always been aware of the fact that these people are an integral part of what makes our sport tick and without them we'd be in huge trouble. And a lot of the people who work at tracks are volunteers, remember, and do it simply for the love of racing and for the love of their local track. They actually create a bit of a feel-good factor in that respect. Or at least, they do with me. They're good souls and having them on my side means an awful lot.

The timing of the jockey's presentation varies each year and because there are always so many other presentations and official events going on throughout the day, the intervals between each race are much longer than usual. This just adds to the pressure as far as I'm concerned (I've never enjoyed long intervals between races) although as long as I've plenty to do I'm OK.

The only thing that can really augment being crowned champion jockey is you having some success on Champions Day itself. This has always eluded me in the years I've won the championship and although I was hopeful of breaking my duck this year, sadly it wasn't to be. Flora Of Bermuda in the Sprint Stakes overperformed to finish third, but Tamfana in the QEII disappointed by doing the same. She ran a great race but the ground was very slow and she was up against the colts. I really thought she could win, though.

The icing on the cake with regards to the occasion of today was having my family present. As champion jockey I get a free hospitality box, and they all came over from Ireland

and made a day of it. Uncles, aunts and cousins from both sides of the family. They really enjoyed themselves. Nothing would have given me greater pleasure than to pop up to the box and see them all after a race having won it, but you can't always get what you want. In fact, I'd probably have to blame them for a lot of the pressure I was feeling!

In all seriousness, my family has always stuck by me no matter what and have seen me rise, fall and now rise again. Success has never been a condition of their support, of course, but to achieve it again after having put them through so much worry and anguish is gratifying. It's the proverbial happy ending for me. And for them, I think.

Despite what the person at Ascot said to me as I was arriving this morning, the act of actually lifting the champion jockey trophy was never part of my motivation. In fact, if they decided to melt it down and turn it into an ashtray or something it wouldn't bother me in the slightest. What the trophy signifies is all that matters and knowing that I'm top of the table on the third Saturday in October is all the reward I need. The trophy could be ten feet high and made of solid platinum but it wouldn't make any difference.

In my early days as a jockey I used to lie awake at night dreaming about how it might feel to lift the trophy. Then, when I did, I didn't feel very much at all really. I've always been a bit jealous of those who do feel something in that situation. Elation, or whatever. I remember watching Chelsea win the Champions League final. One after another the players lifted the trophy above their heads and it really seemed to mean something to them. Why not me then? Maybe one day it'll come to me. Then again, I think it might be a bit late, don't you?

At the risk of sounding like a complete curmudgeon, I actually enjoy Champions Day a lot more when I go there just as a jockey and not as champion jockey. As well as the six races on the card I've got the Breeders' Cup next weekend to think about, not to mention Hong Kong at the beginning of December. I also found the presentation itself a bit embarrassing this year. The jockeys who aren't being crowned champion always form a guard of honour for who is and as they stood there earlier I couldn't bear to make eye contact with any of them. As opposed to feeling proud and like a champion I felt almost humiliated somehow. Like I didn't deserve to be there.

The only anomaly was in 2021. Despite having won the title I knew I was facing a long ban and my future was uncertain. I had no idea if I'd ever ride at this level again, let alone win another championship. This enabled me to enjoy it for what it was and soak up some of the glory but since then it's been anathema to me. I don't know how to handle it and I don't know how to enjoy it. I apologize for sounding so negative but that's the way of it.

Anyway, there's no rest for the wicked. I've got two long shots at Longchamp tomorrow (one for Andrew and one for Ed Walker) and then five or six at Southwell on Monday. You see what I mean about not having time to reflect and enjoy your achievements. The presentation aside, I am actually quite proud of the fact that I've managed to regain the title. Then again, I'll have plenty of time to reflect on that when I retire. For the time being, there's a bit to be getting on with.

TUESDAY, 22 OCTOBER 2024

Lambourn

I just thought I'd check in and give you a quick post-Champions Day update. I was also a little bit preoccupied on the day and forgot to mention a few things.

After a small bowl of porridge, I had counselling this morning between 9am and 10am and in a second I'll be off to the shops to buy toothpaste and orange squash. After that I'm going to drive to Ascot to pick up the trophy. I haven't told anyone that I'm thinking of melting it down and turning it into a very expensive ashtray yet. Anyone interested in buying it? They could actually deliver it if I wanted but I think that would be disrespectful. I might not be that enamoured of it but I don't like the idea of it arriving at my house via a courier. In addition to this, we're having a family dinner at The Pheasant in Lambourn tonight and if the trophy isn't there to show off I'll be in loads of trouble.

I had a good chat with Andrew yesterday. Normally our conversations last about a minute or two (even less over the phone) but this one went on for at least five minutes. He sounds tired which isn't surprising. He's had a good year though and Kalpana winning on Saturday was great for him. As well as getting another Group 1 to add to the list it'll help to keep him at the forefront of Juddmonte's thoughts.

I've been having a think and after the Breeders' Cup I might go to Mexico for a week. There's a five-star show-jumping event there that I want to attend and the plan is to have a day or two either side for a holiday. Whether I'll go or not is yet to be decided. They say that a week is a long time in politics. Well, in racing it's a lifetime.

If I do decide to go I'll be straight on a plane to Bahrain when I get back for a Group 2. Then, on 30 November, I'll have a Group 1 over in Johannesburg. I've never had a winner over there and if I manage to succeed it'll be a great end to the year.

SATURDAY, 2 NOVEMBER 2024

Del Mar, California

This has been my third day in a row of 8st 8lb. I actually felt pretty good yesterday and I'm fine today but Thursday was just torture. My body ached and I felt down and lethargic. On Monday when I arrived I was 8st 12lb (or even a fraction heavier having just got off the plane) and from Thursday onwards I needed to be 8st 6½ every day (stripped naked) to make 8st 8lb. It was such a hard process. I spent every day including Thursday either walking around with a sweatsuit on or lying in a hot bath. The only relief I had was getting into the pool which cooled me down and regulated my heart rate before I went racing. There are sweating facilities at the track but in this case I prefer to arrive, do my job as well as I can and then leave.

Food-wise I've had very, very little since I arrived. Just some salad and a bit of fish every day. For my height and build (I'm five foot six inches and slim) my ideal body weight is probably about 10 stone which means I spend my entire life about a stone and a half under that. On paper, the difference between 8st 10lb and 8st 6½ isn't that much, but in terms of losing that weight and then keeping it off, it may as well be a ton or more.

One high point during the first few days in Del Mar was seeing Frankie. Having been so close to him for so long we always tend to gravitate towards each other. We had dinner on Wednesday with Sheikh Fahad but Frankie also has to work very hard on his weight so there wasn't much food ordered. Despite being fifty-four years old he's still incredibly hungry for success and is very driven.

It should be a bit of a holiday coming to Del Mar but the weights are always in the back of your mind. One saving grace is that the weather has been fantastic which helped to lift my mood yesterday and today. There's nothing like a bit of vitamin D to combat the effects of wasting.

I rode two outsiders yesterday that came nowhere. Then again, both races were a mile on the turf which is what New Century will be racing over in the Breeders' Cup Juvenile later on today. I also have a ride in race four today which is part of the Breeders' Cup undercard. Tomorrow I have one for Charlie Appleby in the Breeders' Cup Fillies & Mares called Beautiful Love but that'll be it for America this year.

TUESDAY, 12 NOVEMBER 2024

Lambourn

I had no success at all at the Breeders' Cup which was disappointing. New Century ran well but needed a little bit further. You get over these things, though. Statistically, even Ryan Moore lost over 75 per cent of the races he took part in last season so even the very best of us are used to losing far more than we are winning. I rode well over there, which is good, and there were no mistakes.

Apart from meeting Frankie and Sheikh Fahad for supper I found it very difficult socially at Del Mar. Particularly dining events. The meeting is packed full of them and I didn't attend one in the end. For a start, I didn't really feel like it but the fact that I couldn't eat just put me off completely. The food over there is somewhat plentiful and sitting at a table for a couple of hours at a time having to make conversation with people who are merrily tucking in to half a cow or whatever would have driven me mad. I was also very aware that I was in bad form and didn't want to put that on anyone else. At the end of the day, I have to do what's best for me and if that means being a bit anti-social from time to time then so be it. Nobody gave me any grief over it.

I was over at Woodbine in Canada on Saturday for two races and then Saint-Cloud in France on Sunday for two more. The weights were all light which caused a bit of misery and not one of the four ran well. Because I'm a martyr to my moods this can affect me in different ways, but whatever happens the crucial thing is how I respond to them. Could this be the therapy talking? Quite possibly. It always feels like I don't remember very much about anything but some things obviously stick.

On one side I travelled thousands of miles, had to make light weights yet came away with nothing, but on the other I got to ride four good horses at two different tracks (as in different to what we're used to) in two different countries. There are hundreds of jockeys who'd give their right arm to have an opportunity like that. The point being that there are positives to be found in most situations, providing you're prepared to look. I don't do it nearly as much as I should but I am learning.

This weekend is busy again. I've got Bahrain on Friday where I'm riding a Japanese horse that can win but it's going to be competitive. I've got Newcastle on Saturday for the first two on The Foxes and then Night Raider, and then Madrid on Sunday for one horse in a Listed race that's part-owned by a friend of mine, the former Chelsea footballer Marcos Alonso. How mad is that though. Ten and a half thousand miles traversed by spending twenty-three hours on various planes and at least ten hours in several cars to ride four horses.

Again, I have to try and look at this positively. It's very hard going sometimes, but if truth be known I probably wouldn't change it for the world. Or at least, not at the moment. Imagine if I was scared of flying though.

By the way, I know it's a while ago now, but I've got another update on the Italian situation. You remember I received a fine of €5,000 for an incident that took place years ago but without a stewards' enquiry? I'd originally been advised by a couple of people to just pay the fine and be done with it, but instead I asked the BHA to speak to the Italian racing authority on my behalf and they agreed. After many attempts, the BHA eventually managed to get in touch with them and miraculously they just dropped the fine. It seems to me like they were hoping I'd just pay up, but as soon as the BHA started asking questions it was resolved. I could be wrong, of course, but as far as I know, no dialogue took place between the two authorities and so no explanation was offered. It's called chancing your arm where I come from. Andrew actually ran a horse over in Italy on Sunday but Hayley Turner rode it. I doubt I'd be that welcome at the moment, nor would I wish to go.

It probably won't surprise you to learn that I ended up having to cancel my holiday to Mexico. Well, I didn't *have* to cancel it. I chose to. Because the ride in Canada came up for Sheikh Fahad and Brendan Walsh and because I had 8st 7lb to make I was forced to make a choice. Racing won the day, as always. I haven't managed to reschedule the holiday so far as I've too much on, but that's just the nature of the beast. I'll have to have another look at the showjumping calendar and see what's occurring.

A few years ago I booked a holiday to Thailand and spent about £5,000. As with Mexico, I was really looking forward to it but at the last minute I decided not to go. There was no refund. I lost the lot. It's the guilt that usually gets me. That and a fear of missing out on something. The thought of sitting on a beach or next to a pool somewhere when I should be riding out or racing is too much to bear. I'm sure you must be thinking to yourselves, wow, what a nutcase. It's what racing does to you though. Jockeys are self-employed and regardless of what level you're at if you don't accept a ride there are plenty of other jockeys who will. This makes taking a break from the sport (and I mean a break where you can actually unwind and concentrate on something else) very hard indeed.

Had we an actual off-season like the vast majority of sports do we'd be able to walk away from the sport collectively for a while, recharge our batteries and recalibrate. We don't, though. As Flat jockeys we get exactly one week off a year. But even that isn't sacred. In November 2023, Flat jockeys were asked by the BHA if we would consider forgoing our holiday in favour of some extra fixtures. There'd been a series of abandonments in the jumps racing calendar due to adverse weather conditions and they wanted to fill in the gaps.

The PJA was asked to canvass its members about introducing the extra fixtures and the response was conclusive. Absolutely no chance. The eight-day break in the calendar had been introduced to support the wellbeing of the workforce so the fact that the BHA had even asked the question caused an awful lot of anger among jockeys.

In their statement regarding the response from the PJA members, the BHA had the cheek to make reference to the importance of the break, saying:

> This is vital to support our participants' welfare and protect the opportunity for them to have their break after a busy season of Flat racing, especially following what has already been a period of adding in a high volume of additional All-Weather fixtures.

Over the years, horse racing has gone from being a seasonal sport to an all-year-round juggernaut. Some would try and argue that the increase is simply down to supply and demand. The more cynical among us might counter that by suggesting that it has far more to do with feeding the mouths of certain industries and organizations.

Would the race-going public be able to cope with the sport being seasonal again, with a break of maybe five or six weeks? Of course they would, which would suggest that the reason it never stops is because the aforementioned industries and organizations are making a heck of a lot of money. The BHA and the like will always try and spin it as being for the good of the sport and will say that everyone benefits. Others will think differently.

I vaguely remember when racing on Good Friday was first introduced in 2014. I hadn't been over in England that long and there was a great deal of controversy surrounding the move. There were two meetings on the day in question, one at Musselburgh and one at Lingfield, and I had several rides at the latter. I remember reading and listening to the arguments from both camps but very few mentioned the effect it might have on jockeys and stable staff. They were never a consideration. Or never seemed to be.

While I appreciate the importance of growing the sport and giving the public what they want, a lot more of the same (and often of poorer quality), which is basically what constitutes the growth in racing over recent years, can often have an adverse effect. Sometimes less is more.

MONDAY, 2 DECEMBER 2024

Lambourn

You might be relieved to know that this is where I've decided to bring the book to a close. There are a couple of reasons for this, the main one being that I've finally made a decision about next year. I'll come on to that later. Another reason is that over the last few weeks I've felt better than I have in a very long time and I'd like to finish things on a positive note. It can't have been easy sticking with me through all my highs and lows so it's the very least I can do. It also won't last forever so I'd better close it now before I go the other way. And I will, eventually.

I had twenty-four hours in Paris last Wednesday with my girlfriend, Lizzy. We had dinner in the Ritz and the weather was on our side. It was just perfect. There's something mystical about Paris at this time of year, especially when it's clear and crisp. On Thursday morning I was brought back down to earth with a thud as I had 8st 7lb to do in Johannesburg on Saturday. The Lord giveth and the Lord taketh away. A few months ago this would have hit me hard having had such a good time, but due to my mood being quite good at the moment I was able to take it more in my stride. After all, it's nothing that I haven't done plenty of times previously.

Being back in Johannesburg felt really good. The last time I was there four or five years ago, the levels of poverty during the beginning of Covid seemed off the scale whereas it didn't seem as bad this time. According to the fella who collected me at the airport, employment has been growing and there's a bit more stability. It's really good to see.

The race I went over there for was the Betway Summer Cup which is Africa's richest race. It's worth 6 million rand in total prize money which is the equivalent to about £260,000, and over half of that goes to the winner. That's a lot of money for a country where horse racing has been in the doldrums in recent years.

In addition to taking part in the Betway Summer Cup and three other races including a Group 2, I was invited over to help promote the sport and I must say they went to an awful lot of trouble. When I got off the plane I was taken to a huge press conference where I appeared to be the main attraction. I was very flattered. The billionaire Mary Slack, who is known over there as the first lady of South African racing, has invested a huge amount of money into the sport, as have Betway. I actually had lunch with Mary Slack yesterday as well as Laurence Michel who is the CEO of Betway

South Africa. Laurence explained that only 1 per cent of Betway's current turnover in South Africa comes from racing. That's now starting to change very slowly and there were over twenty thousand people at the meeting on Saturday. There isn't a lot of TV coverage at the moment and if they can crack that they'll be on to a winner. There's an awful lot of potential in South Africa and I'm looking forward to going back in the new year.

On Sunday I went up to my Uncle Jim's in Leicestershire to go hunting. It was a bit of a family day out really. Jim's daughter Eliza was there and my cousin Claudia flew over to spend the day with us. It wasn't fantastic weather-wise but I rode a beautiful horse. It felt strange not picking up the phone for a few hours.

When I arrived home last night, Lizzy cooked dinner and then I had, wait for it, eleven hours' sleep. I'm not sure that's ever happened before and I feel on top of the world today. Lizzy and her mum and I are meeting a friend of ours for lunch this afternoon and then Lizzy and I are going to see the new *Gladiator* movie. I must have watched the first *Gladiator* movie with Russell Crowe at least two hundred times. I'm not exaggerating. I can tell you every word before they come out of the actors' mouths.

Tomorrow, normality will resume as I've got eight rides at Kempton but I'm almost looking forward to it. Not quite, but almost. Peter Scargill from the *Racing Post* has been quizzing me about next year but I told him that I hadn't made up my mind yet, which is a lie. I can officially confirm that 2024 will be my last championship, at least for a few years but probably forever. My mood is never good for very long but post the Breeders' Cup it's been excellent. For as long as I can remember the first thing I've thought about when I wake up in the morning has been my strike rate or how many winners Rossa, William and Tom might ride and that no longer being the case has been amazing. I knew it had become an obsession but I'd underestimated the effect it was having on me. I forget which morning it was but one day after returning home from the Breeders' Cup, I woke up and I had nothing on my mind. No strike rate, no championship, nothing. It was as though I'd been unshackled from a huge boulder. I felt free. That was when I decided that I'd had enough.

Since the Breeders' Cup I've ridden in no fewer than seven different countries and because of my decision I've been able to enjoy every trip and every race. I've haven't won them all (obviously), nor has every journey or every meeting been trouble-free. The difference is that because I know what's ahead of me, or rather what's not ahead of me, I've been able to stay fully in the moment and just enjoy life a bit more.

A question you might be asking yourself at this point is whether or not writing this book has been a therapeutic experience. I alluded to the possibility in the introduction and promised you an answer at some point. It actually has been quite therapeutic. I have my therapy sessions twice a week but there's only so much we can fit in and this has supplemented that. It's also made me appreciate more than ever just how atypical the life of a jockey truly is. We rarely get a day off (I know, stuck record), we spend our entire professional lives several stone below our natural weight which is obviously incredibly unhealthy, we're judged and presided over by people who cannot possibly comprehend or understand the events or situations they're adjudicating as they've never been there (it isn't their fault but they can't), we're followed by an ambulance while we race and we are statistically more susceptible to drug abuse, alcoholism and depression than any other elite athlete. Yet here we all are. All 450 of us.

I also said at the start of the book that what we do for a living is addictive and I also believe that more than ever now. Given the above, why else would we do it? I'm very lucky as I can earn plenty of money, but the vast majority of jockeys don't and probably won't. We're a commodity. A commodity that makes a lot of people a lot of money. Take us away and that stops. I don't want the public to feel sorry for jockeys, but I would like them to have more of an appreciation of what we go through and what we have to put up with day to day. That was part of my reason for writing the book in the first place and if a few more people get that having read it, then great.

Anyway, it's time for me to stop going on. I hope you've enjoyed it. It's been a bit of an experiment writing a book like this as we obviously had no idea what was going to happen or whether it would even be interesting. It's certainly been eventful, at least for me.

Although I won't be going for the championship again anytime soon, my thirst for success in the saddle is stronger than ever and I'm looking forward to the future. One thing's for sure; whatever happens it won't be boring.

Acknowledgements

I would like to express my thanks and appreciation to the following people: my family, Andrew and Anna Lisa Balding, Sheikh Fahad, David Redvers, my agent Gavin Horne, my manager Jimmy Derham, Bjorn Nielsen, Peter Trainor, my ghostwriter James Hogg, my publisher Henry Vines and my literary agent Tim Bates.

ABOUT THE AUTHOR

Oisin Murphy grew up in Killarney in Ireland. He started riding ponies from the age of four and competed in show-jumping before switching to Flat racing. He has won two British Classics and a number of Group 1 races. He has been British Champion Jockey in 2019, 2020, 2021 and 2024.